Journal Spilling

Mixed-Media Techniques for Free Expression

Diana Trout

North Light Books
Cincinnati, Ohio

www.mycraftivity.com
Connect. Create. Explore.

13 12 11 10 09   5 4 3 2 1

Distributed in Canada by Fraser Direct
100 Armstrong Avenue
Georgetown, ON, Canada L7G 5S4
Tel: (905) 877-4411

Distributed in the U.K. and Europe by David & Charles
Brunel House, Newton Abbot, Devon, TQ12 4PU, England
Tel: (+44) 1626 323200, Fax: (+44) 1626 323319
Email: postmaster@davidandcharles.co.uk

Distributed in Australia by Capricorn Link
P.O. Box 704, S. Windsor, NSW 2756 Australia
Tel: (02) 4577-3555

Library of Congress Cataloging-in-Publication Data
Trout, Diana
  Journal spilling / Diana Trout. -- 1st ed.
     p. cm.
  Includes bibliographical references and index.
  ISBN-13: 978-1-60061-319-7 (pbk. : alk. paper)
  ISBN-10: 1-60061-319-5 (pbk. : alk. paper)
 1. Handicraft. 2. Scrapbook journaling. 3. Artists' books. 4. Altered books. 5. Diaries. I. Title.
  TT149.T76 2009
  745.593--dc22
                            2009011438

Editor: Tonia Davenport
Cover Designer: Geoff Raker
Interior Designer: Michelle Thompson
Production Coordinator: Greg Nock
Photographers: Christine Polomsky, Adam Hand

fw
media

www.fwmedia.com

Dedication

Dan, Bess and Jon (in reverse birth order)

I'm so lucky.

Acknowledgments

Susan Cohen, my friend, my sounding board, my cheering section and, so very often, my inspiration. Thank you.

Tonia Davenport and the talented crew at North Light: You are a great team!

Abington Free Library, for supporting my teen journaling program, and to all of you teenagers for your openness and willingness.

Dad: Thanks for the hands.

To all my students: I learn so much from you.

Contents

Jiggy Bird.

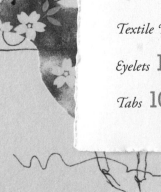

Welcome

Come in and put your feet up; let's chat a bit. First, a warning: I tend to say the most loving and encouraging things in a dead shout. My students, family and friends will attest to this. Oftentimes I forget to be polite and am down-right bossy. Forgive me for my . . . er . . . "enthusiasm" and outspoken-ness. Though I've tried out polite and collected, it just never took.

In *Journal Spilling,* you will find techniques, prompts and encouragement. Pick and choose between the techniques, enjoy them, use and abuse them, make notes right there in the margins—what you learn and what may work better for you. Make good use of the time guidelines; they are in place to help you find the time to journal.

There has been much written over the past several years about using the word "artist" or "writer," to describe yourself. To me, those words imply a "what" rather than a "who." I'm going to suggest that you leave the labels out and simply be a person who enjoys making art and writing. Quite simply, you don't need to be an "artist" to be an art-maker.

Please bear in mind that learning to spill takes a bit of time and trust. It may not happen the first time you sit at your desk or in your comfy chair. Give yourself the gift of time to learn about trusting the process; it's a matter of practice.

Finally, and most importantly, use *Journal Spilling* as a springboard—it is not a box.

Now, get to it! Make some messy journal pages. Go! Skedaddle!

—Diana

Needless to say, you should use whatever supplies and surfaces you desire (and what you have on hand) to make the process of journaling fun and something you will want to return to over and over again. That said, here are some of my personal favorites, and I think you might find most of them appealing as well. Take a look and decide for yourself.

Journals & Paper Substrates

Large Moleskine Sketchbooks (with the periwinkle tab) are cool. I love the rounded edges and the heavy, creamy-colored paper. Yes, the paper curls a bit but I tend to use gesso a lot anyway, which solves that problem. If I don't want gesso, I will glue two pages together to make curling less of a problem. You can choose to not care about curling!

Moleskine's Watercolor Journal is a good choice as well. The paper is pebbly and holds loads of color.

A Spiral-Bound Sketchbook is preferred by many people because it will expand easier and continue to close, even after heavy abuse and collaging. I usually work on two-page spreads in my personal journals, so I don't like the coil in the middle, but I love them as sketchbooks.

Stonehenge is a paper that I really enjoy using because I like a sturdy paper for journaling. If you have basic bookmaking skills, this paper is a good, economical choice. I've had batches that crack a bit when they're folded and that drives some bookbinders nuts. I say the price is right; if it's an exposed spine, put some paint or marker over it. I've used Stonehenge paper for most of the projects in this book. The surface feels a bit harder than the Fabriano Artistico, which is another excellent paper. These papers come only in large sizes, in the neighborhood of 19" × 33" (48cm × 84cm).

Japanese Paper, also called rice paper, is marketed as Sumi-e (*sumi long A*). It can be found in rolls or pads in most art and craft supply stores. It is lightweight and translucent, making it a wonderful collage paper.

So you can see, there are pros and cons to each type of journal. Go to craft shows for local handmade journals or try a bookstore. Seek out an art supply store. Wander the paper aisle and feel the papers. Ohhh, such fun. Ask for help from the sales assistants.

Made-to-order

Consider making a paper sample journal using several different papers that catch your interest at the art supply store. Take the assorted papers to your local multitasking copy shop. They can cut the papers and bind them for you. Make sure the papers are all labeled if you think you might want to purchase them to use again, so you have a reference when the time comes.

Adhesives

Golden's Semi-Gloss Gel Medium is "the stuff." It's a multitasker as an adhesive, and I love semi-gloss to use as a transfer medium. The Matte and Gloss are both nice as well; it just depends what kind of a finish you want.

Gluesticks are simple and efficient. UHU brand is very good.

PVA (polyvinyl acetate) is a "grown-up" archival version of Elmer's.

E-6000 is great for sticking down larger, heavier items.

Elmer's glue works just fine and the smell will take you back to your grade-school days.

Mod Podge is another good adhesive for collage. (It also smells quite nice . . . or is that just me?)

Tapes such as drafting, transparent, fabric and duct tape are all very good to have on hand. If you have space for only one, I'd choose the drafting tape.

Bookbinding Supplies

An Awl is a pointed tool that resembles a needle on a handle and is used to poke holes through paper before sewing signatures.

Bookbinding Needles are blunt and finger-friendly. Tapestry needles are an economical substitute if you can't find the bookbinding variety.

Waxed Linen Thread is a heavy thread with a coating of wax. It is the preferred thread for sewing bindings together. In lieu of waxed linen, you can use beeswax to coat embroidery floss on small projects, such as the mini-books. For the Rescued Book Journal, however, I recommend the real deal.

Color

Watercolor Paints are transparent, not a huge mess and excellent travelers. They can be used with a wide variety of media and are very exciting to use with resists. When wet, they can be lifted, pushed around and allowed to run into the neighboring color to produce values and mixed colors. You can color over a patch of dried watercolor to create a different color. I love watercolors! Winsor & Newton Artist grade are widely available and very nice to use. After the shock of the initial investment, these paints rock. Start with just a few colors and expand from there.

Water-Soluble Crayons and Pencils are activated with a wet brush or any other means of dampening the surface they are applied to. I was never a huge colored pencil person until I found Derwent Inktense watercolor pencils. They are great for drawing, doodling and detail work. Watercolor crayons are gushy, smooshy and wonderful, and my favorite kind are Caran d'Ache NeoColor II (pronounced *karen dosh*—as in, *posh*).

Portfolio Water-Soluble Oil Pastels are inexpensive and can be found in art supply stores and even some office supply stores. They earn another high mark on the "gush scale." Use as crayons for filling in large areas, and blend with your finger or water. It washes right off your finger, but you could use a cosmetic sponge if you've run out of clean fingers.

Caran d'Ache and Portfolio crayons/sticks can be soaked in water first to "juice" them up. You can also run a wet brush over the tip to pick up small amounts of color.

Geek alert: I once did a "highly scientific" experiment to check the lightfastness of Portfolios alongside Caran d'Ache. They *both* held up remarkably well when exposed to sunlight for six months!

Artist Inks are water-based, permanent color. There is a herd of ink brands on the market: reinkers for stamp pads; Ziller Inks; Winsor & Newton Inks; Dr. PH Martin's Calligraphy Colors; and Speedball—all good choices. (I must admit to being a big Ziller fan.) Sometimes opaque and sometimes transparent, while inks often act like watercolors, they aren't typically reactivated with water in the same way and, in fact, most often act as a resist, like the items listed next.

Resists

Art Masking Fluid is a liquid that can be applied directly to your journal page. It needs to dry thoroughly before you apply color. It forms a rubbery barrier that prevents the watercolor from staining your page, allowing you to retain the white (or another underlying color) of the paper. I use Winsor & Newton's version.

Crayons and Oil Pastels (*not* watersoluble) act as a resist to watercolor.

Glaze Gel Pens are another good resist. I prefer those made by Sakura Japan.

Embossing Powders that have been melted by a heat gun also form a resist, with the added quality of providing some dimension.

Drawing & Writing Tools

Permanent Black Pens, such as Staedtler Pigment Liner, Micron and Prismacolor, have a system for the line weight. The thinnest line I've found is .005. The higher the number, the thicker the line. These pens are generally waterproof, but check the label first to be sure.

Colored Pens are fun and available from many companies. Zebra Sarasa are my personal favorites. Many people love Sharpies, which come in a gazillion beautiful colors and a few different point sizes.

Gel Pens are great for white, black and colored pages. I love the quality of all of the pens made by Sakura Japan, and they seem to write forever.

Ranger Inkssential White Pen is the first white pen I've found that really works. It provides a consistent, thin white line.

Copic Markers will write over anything! I have a 2-ended black Copic with a chisel tip and a brush tip.

Graphite Pencils are labeled as HB, 2B, 4B, 6B (as the number goes up the lead gets softer and smooshier). Sometimes you just need a good old pencil, not to mention that graphite is great to sketch with and to blend. Soft pencils will go over a lot of media.

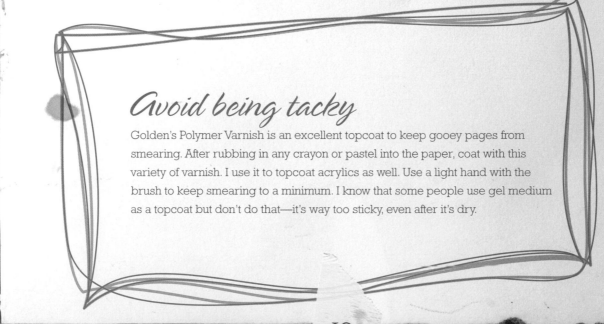

Avoid being tacky

Golden's Polymer Varnish is an excellent topcoat to keep gooey pages from smearing. After rubbing in any crayon or pastel into the paper, coat with this variety of varnish. I use it to topcoat acrylics as well. Use a light hand with the brush to keep smearing to a minimum. I know that some people use gel medium as a topcoat but don't do that—it's way too sticky, even after it's dry.

Charcoal in stick or pencil form provides a wonderful messiness and tremendous depth. I like the soft 6B pencils and sticks for drawing into wet gesso.

Gesso (pronounced *jess-o*) is a white paint used as a primer on canvases. I use it both to prime paper and, thinned, to barely cover writing. I use it on top of Portfolios. You can thin it a bit with water for more transparent coverage. Buy small and see which brand you like the best. As with most art supplies, the higher quality yields a more consistent result. Golden brand is creamy and silky and gives great coverage.

Stamp Carving

Staedtler Mastercarve is a soft printing block resembling a white eraser, and it is very easy on your hands to carve. It is available at most art supply and craft stores.

Speedball Block-Carving Tools are available in a package with one handle and four insert tips. You can usually find more tips at your art supply store.

Bits & Bobs

Bits of collage papers, found papers and ephemera, tags, rubber stamps, buttons, bits of yarn, etc. are loads of fun. I love packs of origami paper; you may prefer the scrapbooking papers, soap wrappers, candy wrappers and so on. Those rub-on letters and decorations are pretty groovy too. Just don't overdo it. Keep in mind the constraints of your space or go shopping with a friend and split stuff up.

← Fez

41

Warming Up

Sometimes you simply don't have the time to journal. You are distracted, you are stressed, blah, blah and more blah. Those hectic times are the best time to give yourself a few moments. Like a brisk walk, time spent with your journal can help you feel centered and energized.

Thinking ahead and organizing your space is the key to spur-of-the-moment journaling, even on hectic days. Suddenly, your journal becomes a refuge because it is always ready to go. Here are some guidelines to setting up your own space.

Consider a small area in your home that you can designate for journaling. A small desk area with a couple of drawers and a bookshelf is ideal. If you have a kitchen table and space for a set of roll-away plastic drawers, you are in business. You can use the storage space under your bed or sofa and some plastic shoeboxes if space is tight. You can get a lap desk and a floor pillow to make yourself comfortable.

Your goal should be to gather your tools and materials in one place: everything down to the glue stick and scissors and a jar of water with a lid. Don't rely on the scissors from the kitchen. Have everything you need right in the area you choose to journal in. The constraints of the space you choose will dictate the amount of materials and tools that you'll be able to store and ultimately use, so take that into consideration when selecting your spot.

Collage Spilling 101

There are three big components of journal spilling: Words, Colors and Collage, and all three will be covered more thoroughly throughout this book.

Flash Flood Journaling Kit

Would you like to get started right now? Are you having a journal emergency? Take five minutes and gather the following materials.

Journal or Other Paper Substrates
Grab any kind of notebook, paper or certainly one of those beautiful blank journals that you currently have collecting dust on your bookshelves.

Pen or Pencil
Does it write? It will work!

Glue Stick
This is simply the quickest, easist thing to glue with. I also like it because it doesn't warp paper, but if you don't have one just yet, any paper adhesive or general-purpose glue will do.

Scissors
Don't use scissors that will frustrate you because they won't cut paper. Find some decent scissors.

Sticks of Color
Crayons, markers, colored pencils—whatever you have and enjoy using.

Paper Scraps
A magazine, newspaper, junk mail or those great collage bits you've been hoarding will all work.

Pile these supplies into a shoebox. This is enough to get started.

Read through this exercise before you start. It is a take on an old, surrealist parlor game, and it should only take 10 minutes to complete.

Time to Spill

1 Open to a random page in your journal. (Don't start on the first page of a brand new, beautiful journal; this will make you nervous.)

2 Quickly now—no thinking—go through the magazine or other scrap papers.
   - Rip out 7–10 pages.
   - Rip down to 7–10 images or text scraps.
   - Drop the scraps onto your paper.

   Don't let yourself stop! Aack, I know that's hard! But hurry through it. That's right HURRY—don't give yourself time to think.

   OK, take a couple of big breaths.

3 Randomly choose a color and, depending on what you chose, scribble or brush the color all over the page. Still no thinking! (*Oh, no! It's a big mess!* Say to yourself: "It's OK, it's just a journal page.")

4 Are any words occurring to you? Scribble them in.

   Write around the collage items.

   Repeat after me, "I don't care what this looks like."

Take pride in messy, murky process pages. This is step one in letting go.

Now that you have gotten your feet wet, you might want to add supplies to your Flash Flood Kit and "soup up" your space to your liking.

Open your calendar and make dates for yourself to take the time to get set up nicely. You can break it up into half-hour segments or take a 2-3 hour block of time to get yourself completely organized.

Remember to look carefully at the space you will be using. You don't want more "stuff" than can be contained in that space. Go through your art supplies. Make a list of what, if anything, you need from the art or craft supply store. Purchase what you need. Unpack and set up your area.

Breaking Down Excercises Into Doable Elements

Seriously now: How much time do you have to journal? Some days 10 minutes, other days an hour? Breaking exercises or techniques down in bits of time that fit your schedule is an important skill to apply to journaling time.

Sark discusses the concept of micromovements in her book *Make Your Creative Dreams Real*. Micromovements refers to a system of breaking down a large job into tiny parts. This is a great concept that addresses the biggest obstacle between you and your journal: Fear. It also helped me greatly with time issues. If you break down a job (or hope or dream), step by step, it seems less scary and overwhelming. I've broken the journaling process down in this way as follows.

You'll find the steps for projects and techniques in *Journal Spilling* pretty neatly laid out. You can break at any point between the steps. If you have your journaling space set up, it will be easy enough for you to open your journal, write for 10 minutes and then paint some gesso or watercolor over the top of it.

Wash out your brushes and refill your water container after you've used them. That way, they are always ready when you need them.

Read over the Techniques sections and you'll find you can break those down as well. For instance, the photo-transfer techniques require that you print out images onto specific papers. Break that down into the following steps:

- Go through your image files on your computer or through your photographs. Is that all you have time for today? Fine.
- Next, scan the photos or if they are already in digital form, organize them into a file on your computer. Time to keep going? Great! If not, come back tomorrow for more.
- Purchase the paper.
- Print the images out.
- Gather the gel medium.

Get the idea? Go ahead and break things down in the book as you are reading through and work at your own pace, realizing that much can be accomplished when you take things a little bit at a time. Don't forget that this is all supposed to be fun!

We took at look at Collage Spilling on page 12, but what exactly *is* "spilling?"

Let's look at the Japanese custom of pouring sake. The sake cups are placed on a tray, and the sake is poured into the cups until it spills over onto the tray. This is a symbol of generosity, hospitality and of making sure each of the drinkers gets a full measure of sake.

This is the picture to have in mind when going through *Journal Spilling*.

Generosity

You can learn to be generous toward yourself. Allow yourself the time to journal and accept pages that are not perfect but rather *real* and true to you.

Hospitality

Your journal always welcomes you. It is, after all, just a book, and it is *your* book. It does not judge "ugly" pages or habits that are irregular.

A Full Measure

In a moment, your life changes. Journaling, for me, is a way of reflecting on those moments—giving those moments their full measure. Turning that moment over in your mind. Dreaming about the future.

For me, it's obsessing over whatever happens to be my current obsession. Today, it may be the color periwinkle or a checkerboard pattern; tomorrow the word *vibrant* may have me entranced.

Now go to it. Practice trusting and being kind to yourself. Practice not having a preconceived idea of what a journal page will look like. Like yoga, journaling is a practice, and is darn good fun in the bargain.

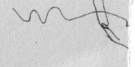

Feet First Into Watercolor

Watercolors are a quick way to get color into your journal. Once you are set up, you can just give them a spritz of water and go.

I find watercolors to be very user friendly, despite the "mystery" that comes along with them. Just approach them as you would any other coloring-in tool.

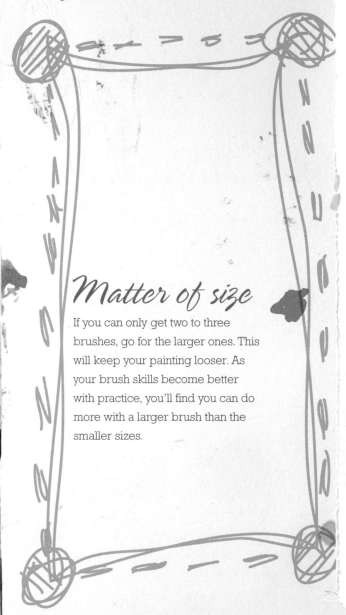

Matter of size

If you can only get two to three brushes, go for the larger ones. This will keep your painting looser. As your brush skills become better with practice, you'll find you can do more with a larger brush than the smaller sizes.

Gather This

plastic paint palette box, folding

journal with heavy paper

small jars of water (lidded), two

paint rag

small spray bottle

old rag

starter watercolors:

    Winsor Yellow

    Winsor Blue (Red Shade)

    Rose Madder

    Lamp Black

    Burnt Umber

optional watercolors:

    French Ultramarine Blue

    New Gamboge Yellow

    Winsor Red Deep

    Cadmium Yellow

    Hookers Green or Sap Green

    Burnt Sienna

watercolor brushes:

    1" (3cm) flat wash brush

    ¾" (19mm) flat brush

    no. 12 flat brush

    no. 12 round brush

    no. 6 round brush

    no. 3 round brush

    no. 4 Japanese brush

    liner brush

Setting Up Your Palette

Plastic palettes are available at art stores. They are fabulous time- and paint-savers. Prep your palette when you have five minutes. If you don't have time to paint right now, leave your palette open and undisturbed for a few hours to let the paints dry before you close it. When you are ready to work in your journal, open your palette and give the colors a healthy spritz of water. The water will seep into the paints, and they will be freshened up and ready to go in a couple of minutes.

1. Squeeze Out Some Color

Squeeze a small amount of color from several tubes of paint onto your palette. Start with the basic Rose Madder, Winsor Yellow and Winsor Blue or as many colors as you like.

2. Add Water

Spritz the paints with a gentle rain of water.

3. Make a Puddle

Wet your brush and swirl some paint into it, adding more water if needed. Here I made a nice juicy puddle of Rose Madder paint.

4. Mix It Up

Mix some colors right on your palette. I made a puddle of blue paint, rinsed my brush, and then picked up some Rose Madder paint and added it into the blue to make purple.

Getting Comfy With Your Brushes

Princeton and Plaid are two brands that make good, economical brushes. I generally prefer the shorter-handled watercolor brushes that have a bit of spring to the bristles. I use these for acrylic painting as well. Don't buy cheap brushes! Those bags of brushes in the craft store are going to drop hairs all over your journal (which is only fine if you are painting a picture of your cat).

Open a random page in your journal and try out a couple of different brushes and brushstrokes. It is fun to do this in your journal so that you can see your progress after you have practiced and played. You can make notes in your journal to refer back to. You may not be happy with your first marks. Have faith: You will improve if you keep at it.

Preparing Brushes to Paint

Give your brush a healthy swish in the water; you want to thoroughly wet the bristles. If you are right-handed, hold a rag in your left hand and the brush in your right hand. Gently wrap the bristles of the brush with the rag to remove any dripping water. Now your brush is ready to receive the color. Go ahead and dip the end of the bristles in water again if you think you blotted up too much water with the rag.

Play around with this until you have the water-to-paint ratio right. The more water you add, the lighter the paint will be as it goes onto your paper. The less water, the more dense and dark the color. (I use this same brush-prepping technique for acrylic paints.)

I always use two cups of water when painting. When changing colors, I swish my brush in one cup and then use the second cup for another rinse. This way, the second cup of water stays relatively clean, thus keeping the colors cleaner.

Protect your brushes

Wash your brushes after each use. Rinse your brush well, put a couple of drops of liquid soap into the palm of your hand and swirl the bristles gently until they are clean. Blot the brush dry, removing as much water as possible and reshaping the bristles. Allow the brush to dry with the bristles upright. (Ideally, the brush should be hung to dry so that water stays out of the ferrule of the brush.)

It's fun to designate two or three spreads in your journal for brushstroke practice and technique. Down the road, you can then use brushstroke practice pages as backgrounds for journal pages. Or, you can also practice on separate sheets of paper and use the papers as collage fodder.

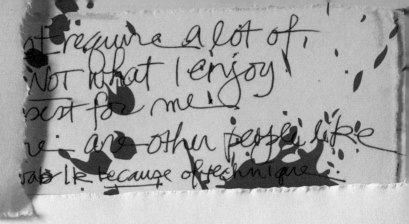

1" (3cm) Wash
This hefty 1" (3cm) brush can be loaded with enough paint and water to color large areas.

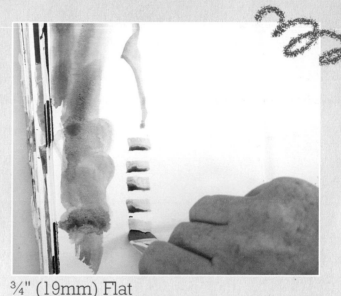

¾" (19mm) Flat
Use this brush to create wide or narrow lines of color, depending on the angle you hold it. If you work on dry paper, the line will be harder. Try with a dry brush and dry paper, and you'll notice the paint skips. This is called *scumbling*.

Round no. 12
A round brush can be pushed down on the paper and pulled back up to create shapes with points on either end. The point alone can also create thin lines.

Flat no. 2
This brush is great for creating small squares or rectangles, or thin dashes. Practice twisting the brush as you move it to see what happens.

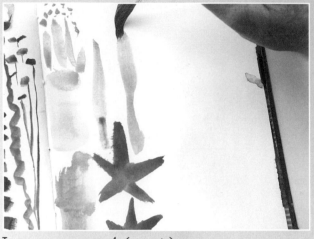

Japanese no. 4
I love these brushes! Load your brush with water and then dip the tip into color for a gradated wash.

Japanese no. 4 (cont.)
Depending on the pressure, you can create very thick or very thin lines and gradual variations between.

Round no. 4
This brush is good for making fine lines or adding small details and writing.

Liner Brush
This detail brush can be used for writing and line work. It holds a good bit of color.

Label Your Experiments
Label your experiments so that you can remember which brush made which marks.

Time to Play

Your journal is the perfect place to experiment! (Here it comes, the words about blank-page syndrome.) Close your eyes and imagine the white page overflowing with rivers of color. Take a few breaths and do it. Just spill some paint. It's OK to just play around with paint or writing or whatever media you like in your journal.

I've seen plenty of blank journals. We don't often get the opportunity to see the journals that are just started and brimming with promise; the journals that are half-full and beginning to splay; the journals full to bursting, spilling over with saved bits of paper stuffed and clipped in, pages overflowing with color, words, images; and the journals with dog-eared pages and pages curling and sticking together.

If you go through one of my journals, you will find some incomplete pages, like unfinished thoughts—messy, ugly pages, but then also beautiful pages that you want to linger in. You'll find pages full of writing and some with art. You'll find pages completely blank or perhaps a page that just has a background color. In this way, a journal really, truly imitates life. It is not a '60s style TV family or an ad with a happy, successful woman wearing a really cool pair of boots. It is wabi-sabi: beautiful and dying; ugly and alive; a perfect vessel with a crack. It has a true, deep beauty like a woman over 50.

Don't think!

Work swiftly when spilling whether in words or images. Try not to think.

1. Throw Down Some Paint

Open to a two-page spread for your watercolor play. Begin by spraying your paper directly with water, just to dampen the paper and make it ready to receive the wet paint. Load a brush and slap it on the paper. See Preparing Brushes to Paint, page 18.

2. Try Blending Colors

Rinse your brush, pick up another color and slap it on there. The colors will begin to blend on the wet page. Pay attention to the new colors emerging. Practice getting that water-to-paint ratio right so that the paint comes furling off of your brush in vivid swirls of color.

River running through it?

Uh oh . . . is your page an ugly mess? Are there rivers, puddles and lakes? Try this: Using a damp brush, lay the tip into the body of water. You'll see the brush wicking up the water/paint. Remove the water from the brush and continue. You can use a sponge, a rag or a dry, cotton string to wick up extra paint.

3. Don't Be Afraid to Experiment

It's alright if you do something that you're not happy with. Here I discovered what would happen if I closed the book while it was still wet and smooshed everything together.

4. Make Notes

If you see something you like, you might want to make a note right in the journal to remind yourself what you did so you can try repeating it sometime in the future. Here, I tried flicking a loaded brush onto the page and then when I went to dry the paper with a hair dryer, it made the paint run in lines, which I liked.

Don't work too hard

If you want to layer watercolors, one on top of the other, make sure that the bottom layer is thoroughly dry. (Use a hair dryer.) Don't overwork the page by brushing and brushing color. Brush the color on and let it go. If your paint is not laying down on the page, it is either because you have too much water on the page or not enough.

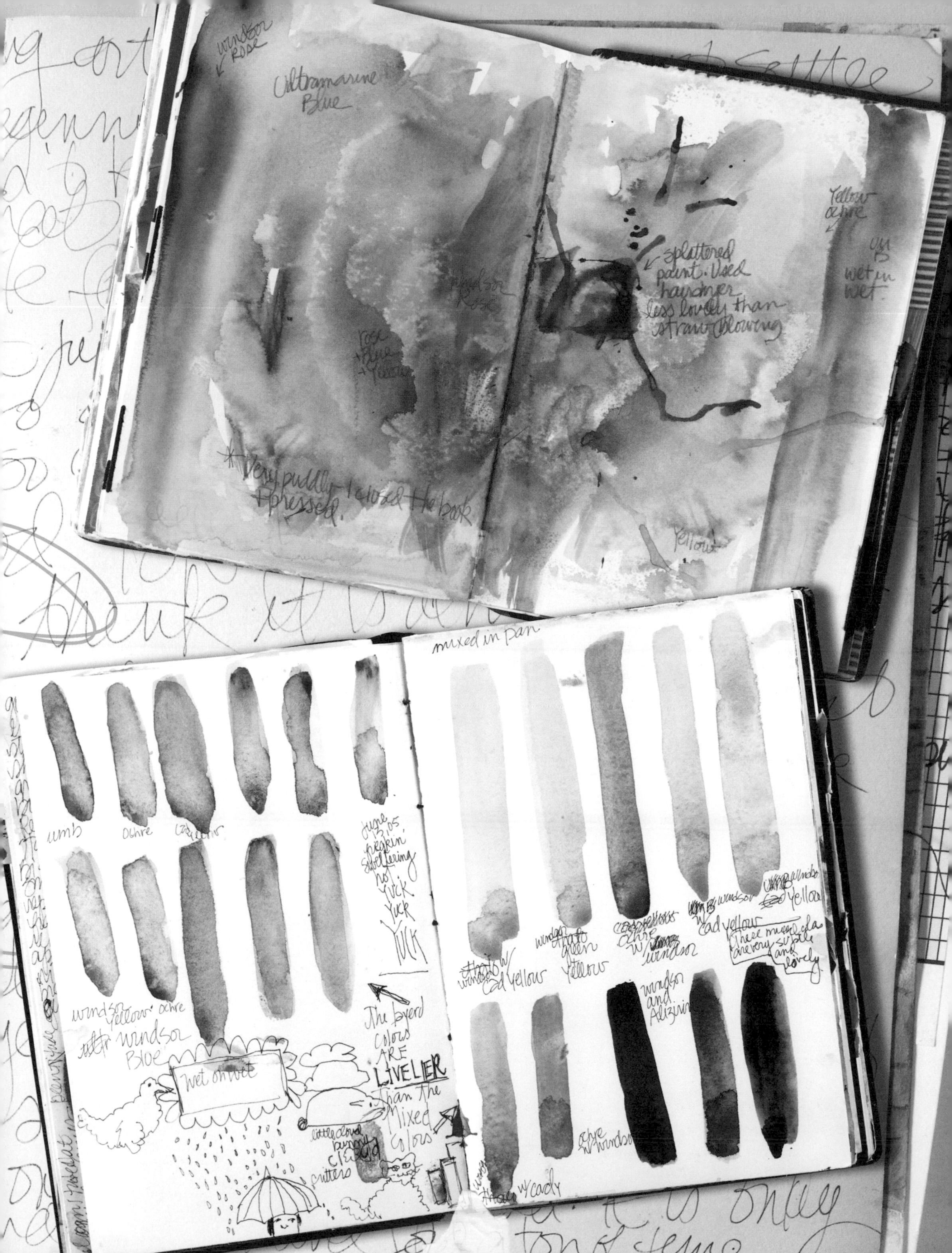

Windsor Rose

Ultramarine Blue

Yellow ochre

Windsor Rose

on wet in wet

↙ splattered paint. Used hairdryer less lovely than straw blowing

rose blue + yellow

Yellow

*Very puddly. I closed the book + pressed.

mixed in pan

umb   Ochre   [color]

June 3.05 pigskin sweltering no YUCK YUCK YUCK

windsor Yellow ochre

ultr windsor Blue

Wet on wet

The pured colors ARE **LIVELIER** than the Mixed colors

little cloud bunny cloud critters

windsor Cad Yellow   windsat green yellow   [color] ochre windsor   new by windsor Cad Yellow   [color] windsor Yellow   these mixed are very subtle and lovely

windsor and Alizirin

ochre windsor

windsor w/cadly

I CAN NOT TRUST small steps

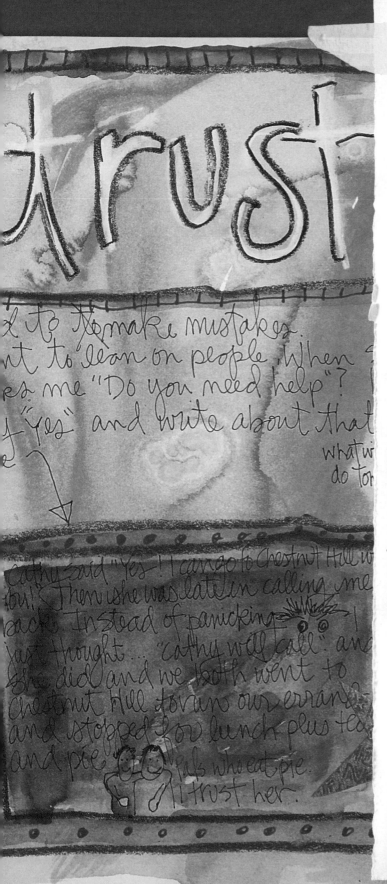

Lean Into Trust

Now, we all know that we are supposed to play and not be afraid to experiment and trust in the process. Sounds like a lot of pressure to me. I don't know about you, but growing up in the '60s with a houseful of kids didn't really set me up to make a big mess and not worry about it. So let's take it slow.

Have you felt apprehensive about getting started in the art-journal process? What is the biggest issue for you, underneath the cost of supplies and the time it all takes (insert personal whine right here)? When you come right down to it, I bet it's *trust* and that darned white page. It's difficult to get over it by telling yourself that's what you need to do.

Think about this quote from Pablo Picasso: "Every act of creation is first an act of destruction." Wow. To create artwork on a journal page, you must first destroy the perfection of that white page. Just think about it though. What would make you stop and look? A blank piece of paper or a paper filled with words and images (even if those images are a bit messy and not exactly what the artist/writer intended)?

Give yourself time to build trust or to "lean into it." Let yourself slowly lean a bit further each time you pull out your journal.

Trust

Gather Your Thoughts

If using a timer, set it for 15 minutes. Take a couple of breaths and, permanent pen in hand, begin to write, scrawl, scribble, spill. Go as quickly as you can. If your mind is a blank, follow Julia Cameron's advice and write "my mind is a total blank." Keep your pen moving. I was thinking about my difficulty with trusting. If something else begins to surface as you are writing, go with it. There is more about spill writing on page 41.

Ding! How was that? Remember that the more you play with or practice spilling, the safer you will feel and the looser you will become.

Too revealing?

It is difficult at first to feel really free about writing your deepest, darkest thoughts. You could write on a piece of loose-leaf paper and tuck it into a secret pocket in your journal. If you do write it in your journal, cover it with a layer of gesso—nobody can see it then, but you will know what it says. Or, write in watercolor pencils and wash over it with water, leaving just color.

There is more about spill writing on page 41.

Gather This

journal

large wash brush

small spray bottle

watercolor palette

cups of water

rubbing alcohol

watercolor pencils

watercolor crayons (optional)

white oil pastel

crayon (not water-soluble)

correction fluid or white paint pen

gel pens (optional)

gesso or white paint (optional)

markers (optional)

permanent pen

gold star

timer (optional)

Color Spilling

1 Pull out your big wash brush and prepare your brush (see page 18, Getting Comfy With Your Brushes). Use a spritzer bottle to spray water over your palette and to thoroughly dampen the surface of the paper.

2 Slap some paint onto your page spread. Randomly spread the paint over some areas of the damp paper. Rinse the brush in a second cup of water and pick up a new color. Spread that over areas of the paper—some new and some to mix in with the first color.

3 Continue rinsing and adding color until you have the amount of color you like. I used Winsor Red, Rose Madder and Cadmium Yellow here to spill color over the page.

4 Spritz the paper with additional water to make it run together in places. You can also hold the paper up and let it run/drip for variety.

Alcohol Spritz Resist

I've varied the background here with alcohol resist. Feel free to sponge, splatter or scribble—whatever you feel called to do. While the watercolor is wet, you can drop alcohol onto it with a brush, and the paint will run away from the alcohol drops, creating a resist. In addition to using a brush, you can also use a spritzer filled with alcohol. Allow your page to dry completely.

This is a good time to take a break!

Simple Words, Big Thoughts

When these pages were dry, I came back and read my writing, thinking about the word *trust*. Simple words, invoking big thoughts, can be created over the top of the spill writing using watercolor crayons, as I've done here. You may have something else you are writing about. I wrote the word *trust* in big letters with a white crayon. You could use oil pastel or regular crayon (not water-soluble) for a crayon resist, too. (See Trust techniques, page 32.)

Boxes & Borders

I default to drawing boxes, circles, little houses, flowers, anything to keep myself moving. Here, I put in some boxes and steps to define spaces to write in. I've also written a little story that illustrated my need to trust, not only in myself but also in others. I set myself an assignment: I would seek out an opportunity to allow myself to trust someone when I may not have before.

Leave an open space (here, a defined large box) on the spread where you can fill in the results of a personal assignment later.

Keep Spilling **Trust**

After I wrote the story of my non-trusting ways, I gave myself an assignment: The next time someone asks me if I want some help, I'll say "Yes." The next time I need to believe someone will do what that say they will, I'll trust. Think about an appropriate assignment you can give yourself and spill away.

Define & Add Depth

I looked at my page and decided I needed some more dark and light areas to attract the eye, so I used a dark-colored watercolor crayon and some correction fluid to "pop" the words a little for more contrast. You could also paint on some gesso or white paint or use markers. After coloring in some areas with a watercolor crayon, I went over those areas with a wet brush to blend the colors a bit.

Acknowledge Your Results

Gel pens are a fun way to call attention to my "assignment results" box. You may want to draw or color with the watercolor pencils or regular pencils. Do what seems to make sense to you—trust yourself.

Have More Fun With Color

I like to soak my watercolor crayons in a small puddle of water to soften. You can use your wet brush to pick up color directly from your watercolor crayons. Using the watercolor crayon with a brush is helpful when you want to fill smaller detailed areas with color.

Revisit Down the Road

This page spread may be one you come back to, but try not to delay your "mission." Keep it fresh in your mind. After you've completed your assignment, give yourself a big gold star! I gave myself this star after completing part one of my assignment. Part two is going to be harder to accomplish, but I can do it!

Leave some space to journal after you've completed your trust mission. Perhaps you'll want to give yourself another mission.

Act of creation Begins
with The Act of
DESTRUCTION

Acts of Destruction

Every act of creation is first an act of destruction.
—Pablo Picasso

This was a process page where I tried not to think of an end product, but merely did what occurred to me next.

On a two-page spread, I scribbled with Caran d'Ache randomly. I was destroying the white page. I also destroyed some very pretty origami paper by tearing it and dropping it, then gluing the pieces where they dropped. No thought was given to placement.

Try this act of destruction yourself. Do anything that you'd like. Just destroy the white page and don't think about what is coming next—focus on destroying the white.

I poured some gesso over the scribbled crayon and spread it hither and yon.

I began to write into the gesso with charcoal. I wrote large and messy: *Act of Destruction*.

At this point, I just let the page dry.

When everything was dry, I poured some acrylic paint onto the page and banged it around a bit. I wrote again with red paint: *Act of Destruction*.

I thought about what is destroyed in the creation of art and beauty. I thought about the perfect stillness before an orchestra begins to play. I thought about tiny perfect seeds that erupt with roots and stems to form flowers—so much larger than the seeds. (Now, there's a metaphor, right?) I wrote about these things and then painted some flowers on the page.

I blocked out a rectangle with gesso and wrote my quote in the rectangle.

Try it yourself. Try to persuade yourself that it's OK to have no plan when you are going into your journal.

Lean Into Trust

The Techniques

Here are some techniques for you to play with to vary your watercolor backgrounds. Go ahead and play in your journal or on loose paper. You can use the journal pages as backgrounds or loose paper as collage fodder.

Take a few minutes to gather your supplies for these techniques and come back when you have a half-hour or an hour to play—more if you have it.

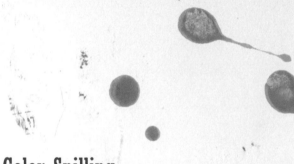

Color Spilling

Work quickly when you are spilling either words or color. The idea is to *not* think. Keep moving and don't let your mind catch up with your hand. Yes, indeed, you will make a bloody mess sometimes.

Gather This

watercolor palette

your journal

spritzer bottle

wash brush

containers of clean water, two

paint rag

rubbing alcohol in a spray bottle or a small dish

coarse or kosher salt

fine sandpaper

art masking fluid (Winsor & Newton)

hand-carved stamp or simple stamp (no small details)

flat brush

regular crayons or oil pastels (not water-soluble)

gel pens (Sakura Glaze)

1. Spray Paper
Use a spritzer bottle to spray water over your palette to refresh it. Use the spritzer to thoroughly dampen the surface of the paper as well.

2. Load Brush
Dampen your wash brush by dunking it in water, then blot it. (See Preparing Brushes to Paint, page 18.) Pick up some paint and work it into the brush. Here, I used the primary colors: red, yellow and blue.

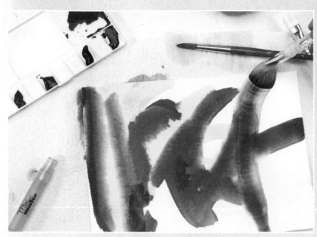

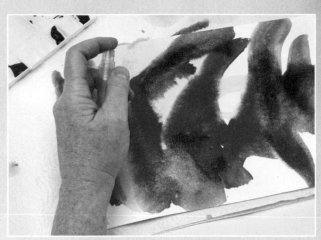

3. Lay Down Color

Randomly spread the paint over some areas of the damp paper. Rinse the brush in a second cup of water and pick up a new color. Spread that color over areas of the paper. You'll see the colors begin to blend and run together on the wet paper, resulting in orange, purple and green. Let your focus be on the page, watching the colors swirl and blend: It's hypnotic. Continue rinsing your brush and adding color. The only way you will learn to be aware of when to stop is by going too far. The colors will become muddy and grayed, the paper too wet, and color will stop sticking to it. That's OK. Let that happen so you will know just how far you can push it.

4. Spray More Water

Feel free to spritz the paper with additional water to make it run together in places, hold the paper up and let the water run and drip for variety. Whatever occurs to you, do that.

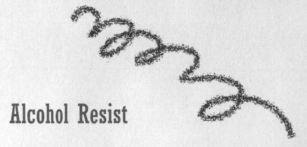

Alcohol Resist

I love resist techniques. They seem like magic, don't they? There is something about the word *resist* that I can really relate to. In this example, everyday rubbing alcohol repels water and gives a unique effect.

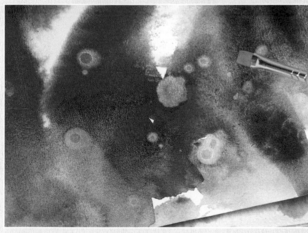

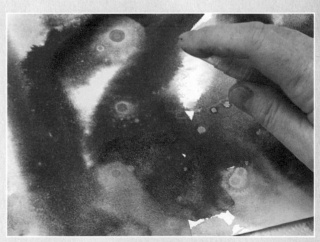

1. Add Alcohol With Brush

While watercolor is wet, you can drop alcohol onto it with a brush, and the paint will run away from it. Very entertaining, indeed!

2. Add Alcohol With Spritzer

Try spraying the alcohol from your spritzer for a different look. This gives a more mottled look, depending on how fine a spritzer you use. If you don't see any results, your paper may be either too wet or too dry.

Salt Resist

Coarse or kosher salt works best for this technique because of its chunkier size. Try varying the concentration of salt from one area of the paper to another.

1. Sprinkle Salt

Salt can be sprinkled onto wet watercolor to soak up the color and create a resist.

2. Rub Off Dry Salt

Let the salt stay on the paper until the paint is dry and then brush it off. A piece of fine sandpaper works well to remove subtle traces.

Masking Fluid Resist

Masking fluid is great stuff. A small bottle goes a long way. It can be a trial to clean up, so be meticulous about cleaning brushes and stamps with warm soap and water along the way. The fluid can be painted directly onto paper to create designs, patterns and words. Using a damp brush, dip into the fluid and write or draw directly onto your paper. Clean out your brush every couple of minutes to make sure the fluid doesn't "clog up" the bristles. In the scheme of play, this technique is best saved for last, so that you can leave it to dry overnight.

1. Load Brush or Stamp

This fluid can be painted directly onto the paper. You can create letters or shapes with it. You can also apply the masking fluid to a stamp. Simple stamps are best to use, since the fluid can be more easily removed during washing. Avoid stamps that you cannot soak. Using a damp flat brush, paint some masking fluid onto your stamp.

2. Stamp With Fluid

Immediately stamp with it onto the paper. Repeat as desired. Clean your stamp immediately and if there is residual "goo," rub it away after it has dried. Let the fluid dry completely on your paper—several hours is ideal.

3. Apply Wash of Paint

Do some paint spilling right over the paper with the resist stamps, and you'll see how the dried fluid resists the color. Washes of dark color are great for a high contrast.

4. Rub Off Dried Fluid

When the paint is dry, rub off the glue-like masking fluid using your fingers. Once you get a little ball of the dried fluid moving, it becomes easier to remove it.

Crayon Resist

There is nothing so comfortable as the familiar crayon; just opening the box and taking a sniff will release some of the fearless 5-year-old from your soul.

Can't top this

Bear in mind that you won't be able to use a regular pen, pencil or ink over the top of the crayon—it will restist those too. So it's best to use crayon resist as a final layer for a journal page, perhaps after some writing or drawing. Collage can be applied over the top of a crayon-resist layer, of course.

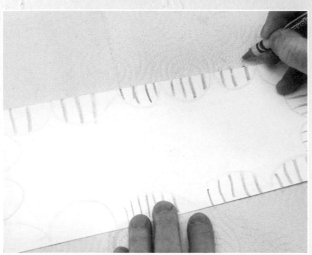

1. Lay Down Color

Doodle, write or color in stuff. The crayoned areas will resist the watercolor. I've created a patterned border and written the word *relief* in pink crayon. This is a nice way to create a border around a page too.

2. Add Additional Colors

Use as many crayons as you like, but stick to the lighter colored (or white) crayons for the best contrast.

3. Paint Over Crayon

Paint over the crayon with juicy, wet watercolor, and you will see it resist the paint.

4. Add Additional Watercolors

Remember, you don't need to stick with one color. Try adding different colors of paint in different areas.

Gel Pen Resist

I love Sakura Glaze pens. They come in beautiful colors and last a good long time. When you write or draw with them, you will see that the line is glossy and raised. Glaze pens can be used as a resist under watercolor.

1. Write With Pen

Using a glaze pen, draw or write on your page. It takes a couple of minutes to dry completely.

2. Add Watercolor

Paint over the dried pen marks, and you'll see the resist. I like to use these in small drawings as well. The watercolor stops running when it hits the glaze pen line. I've used a blue glaze pen with orange paint here. Use a high contrast or complementary color for the best results. Clear glaze pens work well, but are hard to see unless you can bounce the light just right off the page!

More to resist!

You also can use clear embossing with rubber-stamping as a resist. Simply stamp and emboss your image as usual. You can also use an embossing marker to write or doodle. Using clear embossing powders, heat as usual to melt the embossing powder. You can proceed with painting a wash of color over your page.

Taming the Critic

Inner critics are tricky little buggers. They sneak up on us at the most inopportune time—sometimes we don't even know that they're there. Here are some clues that your critic is present:

- ◉ You feel that your idea is silly, stupid, not worth the price of materials or time, and you feel that you are not an "artist" or a "writer" anyway.

- ◉ You feel overwhelmed by a project.

- ◉ You are rolling along with a project, doing whatever comes next. Suddenly you stop and say, "Well . . . I was thinking I should do such-and-such next, but maybe I should wait."

Say "Hello Critic" if any of these scenarios rings true.

Working with your critic is an ongoing process. I was surprised to discover my little devil whispering in my ear when I started working on this section of the book you are holding. *Rats!*

One good way of learning to identify your critic is getting to know him or her through the writing and drawing process. Once you've gotten to know your critic a little better, you may want to take the next step.

You may need to fire your critic or, at the least, demote her. You'll do whatever works for you. Take your time; revisit the topic often. I could devote an entire journal to my critic.

Come along for the ride with an open mind.

I kept coming up from a deep sleep last night, thoughts barely turning through that misty grayness.

Sometimes I forget to take the risk. Sometimes I forget to be brave. I hope I remember this in the morning . . .

I've been struggling with my pesty critic lately. Oh, let me introduce you: He's about 5'3", skinny and insistent with big ugly bug glasses (black). He has shorn black hair and a white shirt buttoned to his neck, tightly ironed. Shiny, high-ridin' flood pants so we can all see his thin, white pilled socks and black, well-polished shoes (tightly laced, of course). He's black and white. I love a metaphor.

My critic says, in his nasally whine, that my ART must be labeled: *Meaningful, Thought-Provoking, Important,* etc. etc. etc.

The arrogant creep.

Why do I put my art in this box? I don't have any trouble letting other artists' work be whatever it is—only my own.

Talking this over with friends always helps. One friend just lets me talk and try to work things out. I take a step forward and think, *My art does not have to be BIG ART.*

I temporarily stop working in my studio and use the less intimidating desk in the living room. I pick up my brushes and pens in the odd spaces of time that occur in life, gently coaxing the art out into the light.

It's OK, ART, come on out. I'm basically a pretty gentle soul, my shy, Child-of-an-Idea.

When I talk with another friend, she comments that maybe the best thing is to lose the labels. I mull. Yes. Labeling just puts creative flow into another box when it really needs to grow. Did you know that when you put fish in a tank, the fish grow in proportion to the size of the tank?

Ideas are not always children or goldfish. Sometimes the metaphors fall apart, and an idea is simply an idea that's not going to work at this moment in time. The artistry, as *Dilbert* cartoonist Scott Adams points out, is in deciding which idea is art and which is simply an idea. That's gotta be OK too. But it still needs to be coaxed out of my cramped brain.

In the meantime, I'll start visualizing my new critic (this time, the critic happens to be a "she") wearing a pair of old, soft, faded blue jeans, orange Converse sneakers with cobalt-blue laces and wild stripey socks, a purple chamois shirt, and a green felt Robin-Hood hat with a big fluffy peacock plume with sage polka dots! Is that an earring I see? She'll lean back and listen. Together the two of us will make all kinds of sloppy dreams in the fuzzy otherworld of that zone in which I create art.

After all, my critic is nothing more than an idea (or ideas) that I grew up on. I think I will make her a more personal vision.

Black and white has never been my gig.

We touched on Spill Writing in the Trust project in the last chapter. Let's take it a step further now, remembering that as you practice or play around, spilling will become easier. Creativity, spilling, drawing, journaling … it's all as simple as setting up a routine and making time for it regularly. The more you practice journaling, the more momentum you build, and the cycle continues. When you were in preschool, you probably couldn't write or read; you can now, right?

Julia Cameron's wonderful book *The Artist's Way* introduced me to spill writing in her section on Morning Pages. I don't always use the Morning Pages routine, but it is liberating when I do. My favorite tools for this are an old-fashioned composition book, wide ruled, and Sarasa pens. It is a very smooth pen on a very smooth surface, so the writing glides out. Here's how my writing today went:

eek! Too much in the brain today, let it go away, no I have to start making a list ok, list: get up, drink tea, write, plan the class, straighten studio, paint 1 hour, geez, i just want to spend the whole day drinking tea but of course it would wind up being boring im just feeling overwhelmed just overwhelmed and my brain feels like cramped and too full spill it out im nervous about the book and book group…

And so on.

At first, the writing is relatively neat, and part of my mind is paying attention to such niceties as spelling and punctuation. I am writing from my mind. Then begins a gradual shift, and I am scrawling large across the page, and it is barely legible. This is fine; this is what you want. You want to be writing from the right side of your brain. It might take a couple of sessions before you are feeling really relaxed enough about spill writing to get to this shift from left to right; be patient.

Don't attempt this on the computer; you need a pen and paper. Cameron suggests three pages, and that works well for me. It'll take about 15 minutes. If you only have 10 minutes, just set a timer.

You might want to have a writing journal and pen by your bed. Sometimes, when having trouble sleeping at night, a good spill puts me right out, or if I wake up with way too much on my mind, my journal is there to organize my thoughts and settle me down.

Try spilling with the prompt, *My Critic*, in the back of your mind. Starting a conversation with your critic is best broken down in small bites.

Be flexible. Don't edit yourself. Just let the words flow straight from your heart, to your hand, to your paper.

My Critic

You can easily break these steps down in manageable time bites. Do the writing in one sitting; come back later and try the watercolor. While that is drying, do the self-portrait. Cut it out and glue it in if the water-colored pages are dry and you have time. Come back to finish it when you have 45 minutes or an hour.

Gather This

journal

water-soluble crayons (Caran d'Ache or Portfolio)

6B pencil

scissors

gel medium

gesso (white)

glue

writing notebook or other light-weight paper for collage

Elements of a Self Portrait

start with a oval →

then a column
then two foothills →

Now for the features:

The eyebrows → and the Nose

Eyes

Bottom of the Nose:

Mouth

Add Some Great Hair!

Self-Portrait

1 Begin with a spill-written page using the prompt, *My Critic* (see page 41). Working quickly, loosely sketch out a self-portrait using a water-soluble crayon for its gooshy smooshy line, or a nice soft lead pencil if you prefer. I made a few basic self-portraits in my spill-writing notebook, going over the lines loosely until I was happy with the shapes. I hear you say, "Aack! What?! Draw a self-portrait?!"

OK, calm down and look at the illustrations on the previous page.

You need to draw an oval, held up by a column, resting on top of a couple of foothills—easy enough, right? Practice this a couple of times. Try using your whole arm to draw, not just your hand. Get your arm moving and draw around the shape until you are happy with it. The art police will not come and arrest you for making a "bad" self-portrait. It doesn't even need to look like you. It could be a creature, a dog, a cat, a bird, a house—whatever you want. Loosely interpret the word "self-portrait."

2 Cut out your portrait shape—loosely. I had sketched out a few, so I cut each of them out. It's nice to have a few choices and then have leftovers for another page.

Place Yourself on the Page

Use Gel Medium to glue the portrait down to a gessoed page in your journal. Go with your gut feeling when gluing your portrait to the page. I glued mine in the middle of the left-hand page on my spread. As it turned out, I wrote around my self-portrait, and it looked like I was in a cloud of words. You may want to place yours higher on the page as if you are looking down on the swirl of words or perhaps lower as if you are being buried under the words.

Spill Color

Watercolor spill around the image. I really try not to plan these spills at all. I simply reach for the first color I see. It is so often red! I never, ever wear red and, outside of my journal, rarely reach for it first. Sounds like I need to do a journal page about that, right? You can add Caran d'Ache to this watercolor layer as well. Just be sure to water it into the page so that you can write over it.

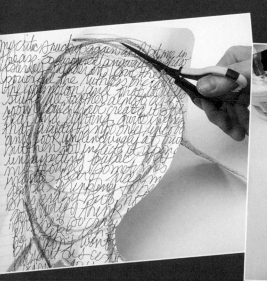

Next, thin down some gesso with a couple of drops of water and apply it on top of the watercolor. I wanted to obscure the writing in the background a little bit. You could scribble into the gesso layer using a pencil or the non-business end of a brush. Add patterns, words, borders or small drawings. Allow this to dry.

Ask Questions

Here, begin writing again, asking yourself questions about your critic. I used a water-soluble crayon. You could use a pencil for this step.

Add Portrait Details

Add some color and small details to your portrait. (Don't panic; details may be loose as well.) I wanted red hair (even though my hair is gray and brown). I gave myself a beaky bird nose too. Your portrait does not have to look like you! I used a water-soluble crayon to outline my eyes and nose; you may want to use a pencil.

Decide on Some Shapes

Maybe you'd like to try adding some shapes to your background? I decided to add some linked circles using a water-soluble crayon. Perhaps I'd write in them or collage? No need to have a plan here. If you think you might want to write inside some of your shapes, try gluing circles of paper in their centers. I added thin rice paper over three of the circles. Again, no real plan needed.

Pick a Word—Any Word

Ah! How about turning to a random page in the dictionary? Close your eyes and pick a word.

Glue the word where your instincts tell you—don't think about it. I glued my word on top of one of the rice-paper circles.

Things that happen when you work intuitively are always so much more interesting. Give it a try and be patient and open-minded.

Identify Your Critic

I really wanted to get a visual on my critic so that I could recognize him. In order to do that, I asked myself (and answered) the following questions. You might find it helpful to ask yourself these same questions about your own critic.

Is my critic male or female? (male)

Does my critic remind me of anyone in my real life? (oh, yeah)

What are my critic's favorite foods? (liver and onions)

Where does my critic go on vacation? (The Wax Museum)

What is your critic's favorite book? (calculus textbooks)

What does your critic wear? (black pants, shoes and tie; white shirt and socks)

What is your critic's favorite expression? ("Tsk, tsk, tsk.")

What is your critic's favorite breakfast food? (black coffee, Wheaties)

How many pillows are on your critic's bed? (one very flat pillow)

What color is his/her kitchen? (white)

Does he/she have any hobbies? (balancing his checkbook)

You get the idea. Go ahead and write down a bunch of questions. They could even be multiple choice such as:

Where does my critic live?
a) Rural area
b) Suburbia
c) In an apartment just off the Jersey Turnpike so he can easily get to work in the morning

What is your critic's favorite color?
a) Hot pink
b) Turquoise
c) Gray

What is your critic's favorite sight?
a) Daffodils in a spring breeze
b) Flocks of birds swooping around in the sky
c) His computer, searching for the solution to some algebraic equation

It took me a while for my critic's name to be revealed to me. I woke up one morning thinking *Stewie. His name is Stewie.* You may decide to apply a name to your critic more quickly. I waited until it occurred to me.

The Critic's Own Page

You can designate a page in your journal for ongoing critic observations.

1. On one half of your critic spread, in your journal (or on any page you wish), adhere paper or images that you think your critic would like. For me, graph papers and lined papers (printablepapers.net) made a perfect background. I love graph paper and so does my critic. Interestingly, we seem to have a few things in common, and I bet you share some common likes with your critic, too.

   I decided that my page would only be black and white, since my critic is very much a black-and-white guy. I glued some of the different papers I'd printed out as a first layer. I glued a drawing of my critic to the page. Look in magazines or draw a stick figure of your own critic—it won't matter to anyone but you. I stamped "My Critic" across the page and then began writing. Leave some areas open so that you can revisit the page with new insights from time to time.

2. Step outside of your comfort zone just a tiny bit, and apply some techniques that you know your critic might not approve of. It can be very liberating! Here, I used a non-permanent black pen. I brushed some water over the top of the words to blur them, as if they were out of focus. Oh! Messy running ink on that very neat black and white page! Be bold and go for it!

MY CRITIC

He doesn't think
out of the box
He loves lima
beans.

My critic
does not
like
Babies
or the
colors
rolling
in the
grass
or
overlapping

My critic is a
slender, medium
height man, he
always wears
Black & White
He loves numbers
so I gave him
the job of
book keeper in
my business.
New Ideas
SCARE
HIM

He sleeps to 6:30
every day, even
sundays. He
wears flood
pants. He's
neck is dangly.
His socks are
piled and always
falling down.

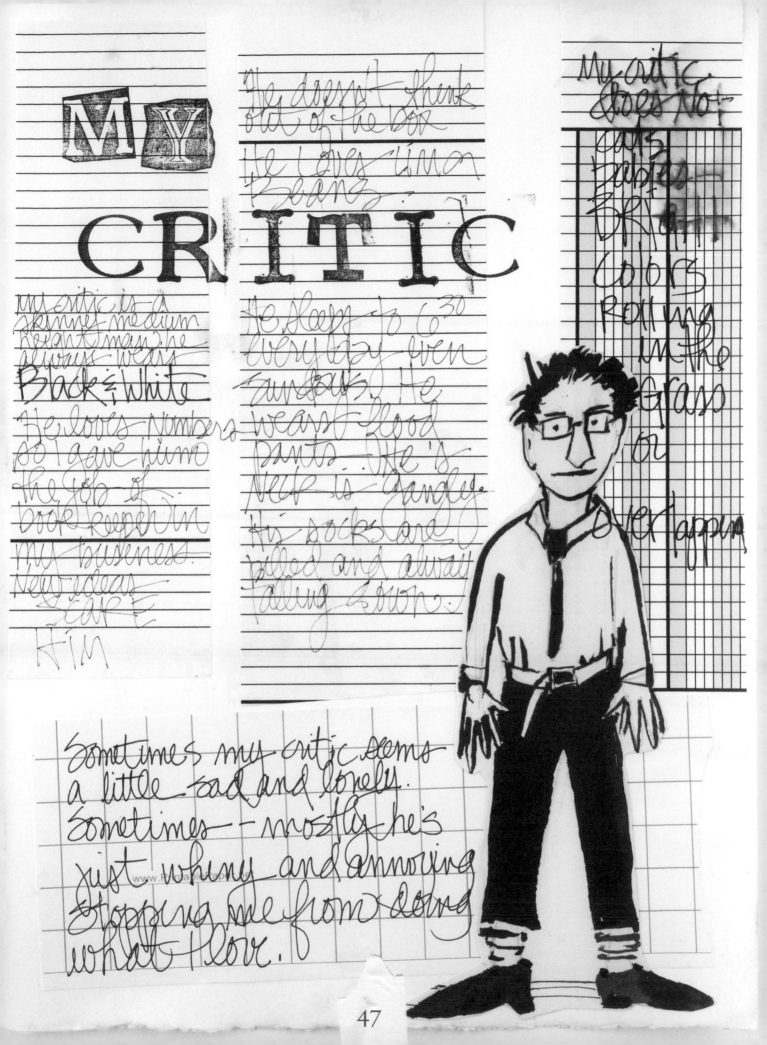

Sometimes my critic seems
a little sad and lonely.
Sometimes — mostly he's
just wheny and annoying
stopping me from doing
what I love.

Taming the Critic

The Techniques

I love to use these techniques because of their scribbly ease; it is a great way to attack the white page. As in all spilling techniques, don't think much.

Gather This

journal

water-soluble crayons

containers of water

brush

gesso

6B pencil

awl

scraps of paper for collage

decoupage medium

gel pen

Gesso & Water-Soluble Crayons

This layered technique has a wide range of applications, from obscuring journaled words in a background just a bit, to creating new words or images on the gessoed surface.

1. Lay Down Crayon
Reach for a random crayon and scribble away. Here I used the warm color family: red, orange and yellow.

2. Spread Color With Water
Spread the color around with a wet brush. Look how intense the color becomes when it is wet!

3. Add Gesso

Add some gesso as a translucent layer. You can still see the color through the haze. Feel free to be sloppy.

4. Write Into Gesso

Roll up your sleeves! It is so much fun to write with a 6B pencil into the wet gesso. Peeks of the first layer of crayon can be seen, and sometimes the pencil leaves its mark as well. Simply wipe the pencil tip off as it becomes covered with gesso. (Wipe it well when you are finished writing.)

5. Scribble in Objects

After writing over the whole page, I decided that I wanted to draw a picture in the middle of the page. Doodle however it suits you. I brushed on more gesso just in that rectangular area and drew into the wet gesso. Yes, that is my kitty. Chopin is a role model of not caring how anyone but her own princess self thinks. She looks at me with one eyebrow lifted, thinking, "Why would you listen to that whiny critic of yours?"

6. Add Additional Crayon

Add more color with an additional water-soluble crayon, blending it with wet fingers as you go. Here, the crayon caught in the hills and valleys created by the writing-in-gesso-layer, creating even more variety.

41

7. Scribe Into Crayon

If you put down enough crayon, you will be able to draw into it with an awl (or other pointy tool). This technique is called *sgraffito*. (That's fancy artist lingo, meaning "to scratch.") It will remove lines of the crayon and allow the under layers to come through.

8. Grab Color From Crayon

With a wet brush, draw color directly off of a crayon and then apply the loaded brush to the paper.

9. Soften With White

If you wait until all is dry, you can use the white water-soluble crayon over the top. I used more sgraffito to give Chopin's fur some texture.

Crayon & Collage

If you're intimidated by collage, here is a good exercise to get you started.

1. Lay Down Crayon

On a gessoed journal paper, lay down a scribble of water-soluble crayons. Here, I used the heavier Portfolios.

2. Spread Color With Water

Spread the color around with water. I love the way this looks; in some areas you can still see the crayon strokes and in other areas, the crayon becomes well blended.

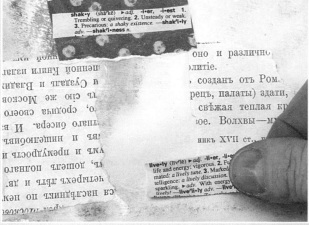

3. Lay Out Paper and Words

While this background is drying, begin flipping randomly through books, magazines or your stack of decorative papers and cut out shapes and images you like. Don't overthink this; just grab whatever appeals to you! Cut a bunch—what you don't use can be placed in an envelope for another time. Lay the pieces over the paper and decide how you'd like them arranged.

4. Adhere Papers

I was fairly deliberate about arranging the papers (I suppose I was designing a bit more than usual), but you don't need to be careful here. I began choosing words that appealed to me. I didn't think too much about them or analyze why I was picking them. The best thing here is to go with your gut reaction. Glue the papers and words down, using decoupage medium.

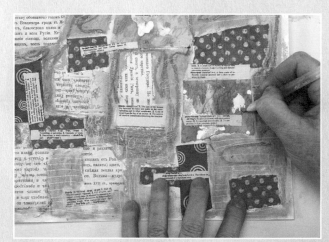

5. Add More Crayon

Apply additional crayon around the edges of the collaged pieces and smear the color into the edges of the paper to make it all more cohesive. You could add a layer of thinned gesso completely over this page if you'd like.

6. Detail With Pen

If you've kept from covering some of your papers with water-soluble crayons, you can now write on them with a gel pen. Journal more about the words you chose to cut out. Also, where the crayon is heavy, you could use an awl to scratch more words or small drawings. You could also add collage elements if that strikes your fancy. Bring an open-ness to this page and see what happens.

Secrets & Wishes

There is so much power in our dreams. I remember lying in bed as a child and teenager, picturing my adult life. Some of my dreams have become a reality. These days, I can still be found dreaming on car trips or in a hammock in the summer. But every once in a while, as I'm going about doing something new to me, it strikes me that some of my hopes that have materialized started in my sleepy daydreams.

About 10 years ago, I began writing my wishes down. In 1999, I wrote, "Make a quilt someday." Just two months ago, I finished my first quilt. In 2003, I wrote, "Admit that I am scared and do it anyway." I remember writing that. "It" was anything I backed away from. "It" was something that I began to look at more carefully and ask myself what would happen if I did "it" and failed? As it turned out, failure didn't seem to be earth-shattering. So attempting "it" became exciting. I began to truly understand the truth behind courage—being scared and doing it anyway.

In the journaling exercise, the *Wishing Quilt*, I hope that you will do a good bit of spill writing. Spill all across pages and fill them up with juicy wishes and dreams. Be gentle with yourself. Coax your dreams and wishes out. Respect the power of the words you write and believe that writing them will fix them into your mind and, maybe, with some attention, some of your dreams will become a reality.

Remember to write your dreams down when they occur to you. You needn't have a special journal page.

Japan

I think I may be a math whiz. I just need the time to find out

diameter · circle · radius

☐ play
☐ stretch
☐ swim
☐ eat myself out the lines

what are my secrets

SECRETS

Wishing Quilt

Every fear contains a wish.

Call on God, but row away from the rocks.

—Italian proverb

Open your journal to a two-page spread. You may also want to have a writing notebook close at hand to begin stream-of-consciousness spill writing.

Scribble, Scrawl, SPILL

Be awash in wishes and dreams. Write it all down—large dreams, small dreams, funny or silly; it should flow from heart to hand to page.

Gather This

journal

water-soluble crayons

brush

containers of water

gesso

pencil

embossing tool

Japanese brush

black ink and/or walnut ink

stir straw or drinking straw

black pen

scraps of decorative lightweight paper (see Suminagashi and Orizomegami paper techniques)

glue stick

needle and thread

scissors

crafting foam or old mouse pad

piercing awl (or thumbtack)

vellum

writing notebook (optional)

objects to add texture (optional)

watercolors (optional)

hair dryer (optional)

sewing machine (optional)

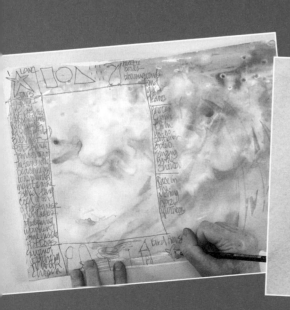

Add Some Color

You've spilled some words, now spill some color. Scribble with water-soluble crayons. I used Portfolio here. I wanted something really juicy, and I kept going over the paper until the color was strong.

I wet brushed the page to further blend the color. Wet brushing also pushes the color into the page a bit deeper so it is not all sitting on the surface of the paper. You could also blend it in with your fingers. At this point, I left the right-hand page of the spread alone. I wanted to create my quilt on that page, so it didn't need any more work just now.

The rest of this process was using only the left-hand page of the spread.

Lay Down Some Gesso

I brushed thinned gesso haphazardly onto the left-hand page, rubbing it off with a paper towel in places. It may seem silly at first to color a page with the crayons and then cover over the color with gesso but it adds immeasurably to the layered feeling. You can add as much or as little as you want, creating some textures. Play with the gesso to see what happens. Press objects—bits of screen, the end of a brush or the top of a paper cup—into it. Draw, doodle. To borrow a quote: "Be one with the gesso, Grasshopper."

Write Into the Wet Gesso

Using a pencil in the wet gesso, I blocked off a box. I thought I'd want some kind of image later in the center of the page, although I didn't know what at this moment. I began to write more wishes and my feelings about making wishes around the box. "Oh my gosh: should I be careful what I wish for?" Not. At. All.

Write Over the Dry Gesso

When the gesso has dried, continue adding your journaled thoughts, writing over the top with water-soluble crayons. Keep the writing and the thoughts loose and free.

This is a good time to take a break and let the page dry.

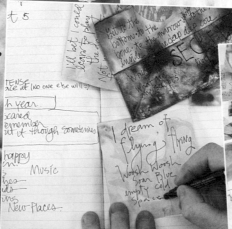

Deboss the Box

I knew that blank space was for something! When it hits you—what belongs in a blank box you created earlier—sketch out your image using pencil. I drew a simple bird shape. Now, take an embossing tool and trace over your sketch lines to create a debossed image.

Fill and Spill with Ink

1   Using a Japanese brush and walnut ink, try coloring in your debossed areas. I began to color in my birdie. Where I had created "dents" by using the embossing tool, the ink settled, creating a feather-like texture. You could use watercolors here, as well.

2   Ink spill! While the ink is still wet, try blowing it around using a straw. This is great for creating branch-like forms or to suggest movement. I sprayed some water into the wet ink so the ink would spread even further in areas.

Take a break to let things dry or use a hair dryer. If there are puddles on your page, take note: The hair dryer will spread them around!

   While your page is drying, pull out your pens, decorative paper and writing notebook.

Stitch on Some Labels

1   On small scraps of note paper, write out your wishes, hopes and dreams—one wish, hope or dream per scrap. Let loose and make a bunch of these; if you don't use them all now, they will make good prompts for another journal page.

2   Using a glue stick, lightly tack in place a couple of your wishes and then begin to stitch them to your page to begin a quilt. You could use a machine here if you like.

Stick it

You don't need to sew at all for this quilt. You could use double-stick tape, glue, staples, regular tape—whatever strikes your fancy. I just love to sew!

Add a Secret Pocket

Don't you love pockets? You may want to tuck some of your deepest secrets inside a private pocket. These are very easy to make! Cut a semicircle at the top of a paper square. Sew the two sides and the bottom to the page, leaving the top open to form the pocket. It's also fun to write little letters to yourself to stick in these pockets.

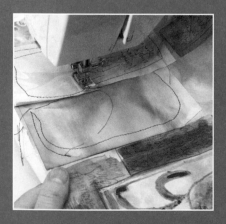

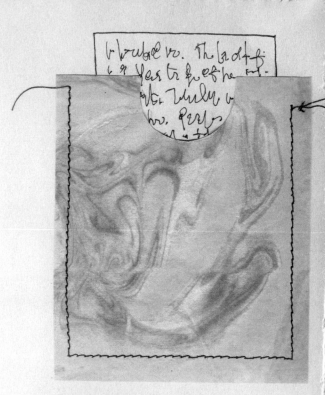

Add Texture With Thread

It's fun to have wiggly black lines around the paper squares on your quilt. I used black thread here to mimic the black pen writing. Use whatever color you like and make whatever sort of lines you like, too—straight, zigzag or a combination of both.

1 You don't want to attempt hand-sewing paper without prepiercing the sewing holes. It's too hard on your hands! Put foam or an old mouse pad down to protect your tabletop. Pierce the sewing holes with an awl or thumbtack in any sort of design you'd like. Thread up a needle and begin to sew. The prepierced holes make this a very simple process.

2 I like to use tapestry needles for sewing paper and bookbinding. With the dull point, you have less chance of piercing or scratching the paper. I have a special affinity for black thread, but use whatever colors you like; embroidery floss is inexpensive and comes in loads of lovely colors. Try dark papers with light threads or metallic threads. Try neighboring colors, such as blue-green paper with blue thread. Twist two different colors of thread together and thread your needle with that.

3 If you are machine sewing, leave your stitch length at approximately setting 3. You don't want your stitches to be too close together as that might perforate your paper to the point of tearing.

Vary your stitches by playing with the settings and stitch length: zigzags, long and short, etc. Any papers can be used for sewing here. If it is delicate paper, such as rice paper, I like to coat both sides with varnish and let dry before sewing.

Finish With a Vellum Layer

To create a final layer for your page, consider adding a transparent layer of vellum. This is not only interesting to look at, but it also serves a practical purpose as well, protecting work that might smear underneath it. I stitched a flap embellished with a sewn-in heart over my page. You can still sort of see what's underneath the vellum, and it easily lifts up. See the techniques section on page 60 for more about machine and hand-sewing paper.

Favorite Things

This pen sewing whup wt
journaling little bad dots
butons reading zines
teaching writing talking
to my peeps Family vacay
Family dinners Birthdays
hearing + telling stories
Drawing painting collaging
Paper Paper Paper Ink
Colors of everything

I wish that I could fast
color like blueberries
and avacado and mango
oh Pineapple everyone b [?]

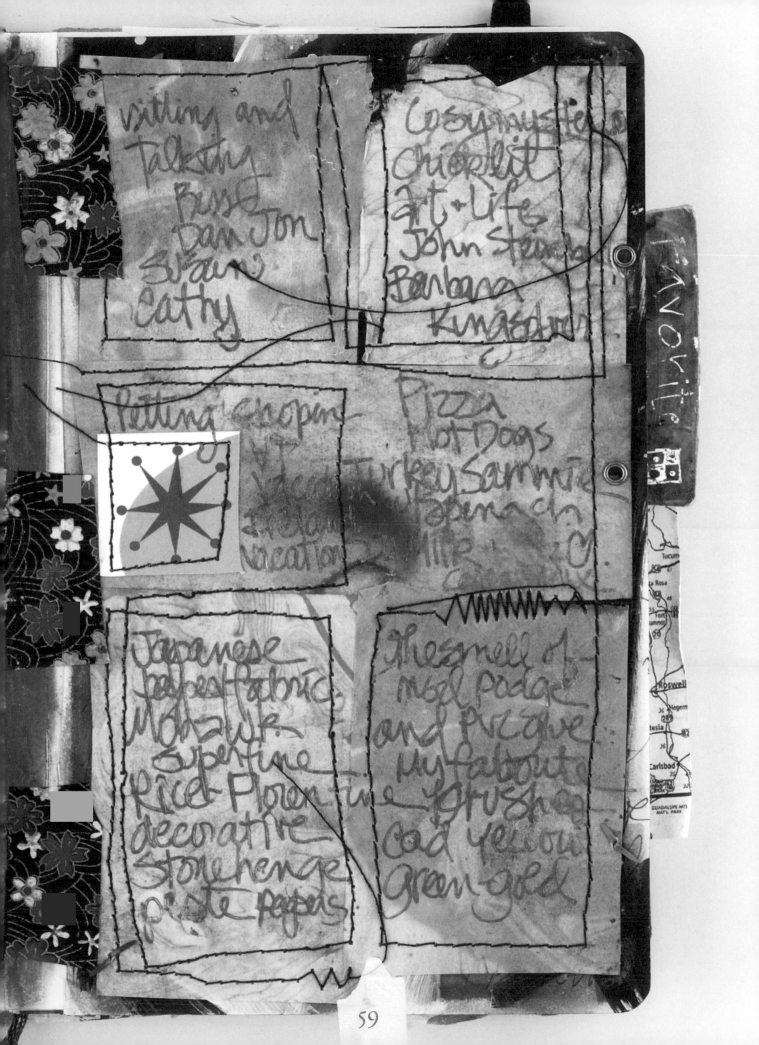

sitting and
Talking
Bess
Dan Jon
Susan
Cathy

Cosy Mysteries
Chicklit
Art + Life
John Steinbeck
Barbara
Kingsolver

Petting Chopin
Pizza
Hot Dogs
Turkey Sammies
Spinach
Vacation
Milk

Japanese
paper Fabric
Mohawk
Superfine
Rice Florentine
decorative
Stonehenge
pastel papers

The smell of
mod podge
and Prizma
my favorite
brushes
cad yellow
green gold

Secrets & Wishes

The Techniques

The techniques for this chapter are among my favorite activities to do, though they may take a bit longer than some others in the book. For the ones that involve ink, you may want to wear gloves. I am always saying, "Well, I'll just do a few papers; I don't need gloves." The next thing I know, there is no standing space in the studio and my hands . . . well, today they are blue with a big red stain on my forearm! Beware.

Suminagashi

Suminagashi means "floating ink paintings" in Japanese. Poetry! Like the name, there is a magical happenstance about this simple process that will suck you right along with it. The papers are the end product, of course, but the process of watching it happen is a reward in itself.

This is messy! Allow yourself at least an hour for this process. Cover your work surface with plastic. I set up an assembly line. Designate an area for dry, clean papers to keep them out of the fray but near the water-filled tray.

Gather This

plastic cover for workspace

tray for water (small acrylic, box frame works well)

plastic "flower" palette or plastic bottle caps

inks: Ziller, Speedball and permanent ink reinkers (deep colors), liquid acrylics

Golden Flow Release (mixed with water as directed on label)

eye droppers or pipettes

Japanese brushes

coffee stirrer or straw

toothpicks and/or skewers

Japanese rice paper (sumi-e)

decorative paper

binder clips

small dish of water

paper towels

water sprayer

embossing stylus

needle

embroidery floss

disposable gloves

newsprint (optional)

iron (optional)

sewing machine (optional)

1. Prepare Palette
Fill your tray or acrylic box with water (about ½" [1cm] is fine). Set up your inks by mixing approximately equal amounts of Flow Release (diluted) and ink in your palette. Also mix some water and Flow Release in the same ratio in a section of your palette. (Have a clean pipette ready to continue adding Flow Release as you go.)

2. Drop First Color in Water
Dip two brushes in plain water, blot and point the bristles. Take a brush in each hand. Dip one into the ink mixture and one into the water/Flow-Release mixture. Just barely touch the water in the tray with the brush filled with ink. The ink will flow off the brush and lay on the water surface in a floating circular puddle.

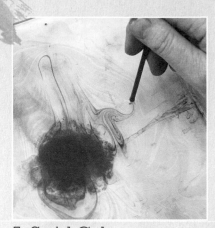

3. Add Flow Release

Repeat with the other brush. The water will spread in a puddle away from the brush, pushing the ink puddle away and into a circle. Continue this until you have 10 to 20 concentric circles.

4. Continue Alternating Ink Colors

I cleaned the blue ink from my brush and added red. You can see that a good bit of the red ink settled to the bottom of the tray here. I made a couple of circles of red ink and water.

5. Swirl Color

Gently blow over the surface of the water, using a straw. You can also use a toothpick or skewer to drag color around and create swirls into a floating ink painting.

Fragile when wet

Rice paper is extremely fragile when wet. You may want to practice this technique with a sturdier paper first. You can use anything from copier paper to art paper. The surface of the paper should be very smooth.

Breathe & release

If the color is sinking to the bottom of the tray, or not spreading, don't fret. You may need to add more Flow Release to the mixture, or your brush is either too dry or too wet.

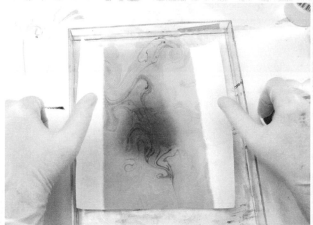

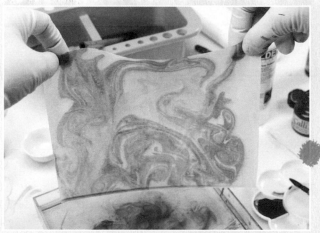

6. Drop Paper

When you are satisfied with the pattern, it is time to transfer! Trim a few pieces of rice paper to be about 2" (5cm) smaller, each direction, than your tray. Take one sheet of paper in both hands. Holding each side, allow it to droop in the center. Let the center touch the water and let go of the sides. Instantly, your paper will become wet, and the ink will be transferred to the paper—rapid magic.

7. Remove Paper

As quickly as you put the paper down, pick it up, allowing the excess water to run off. Dry flat on newsprint or hang to dry. Note: After two or three prints, your tray of water will become muddy. Dump out the muddy water and refill with clean water.

Orizomegami

Orizomegami is another Japanese method of creating decorative papers using inks. The papers are folded to create resist patterns, much like tie-dye. I love this technique, despite the messy hands. It is worth every bit of it when you finally get to open the packet! Each one is always different with unexpected results. This technique is not quite as "fussy" as Suminagashi.

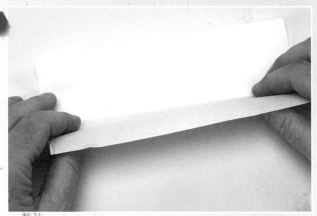

1. Make First Fold

Set up your palette: Using a pipette in each ink bottle and one for the water, squirt ink colors in the palette wells. Add approximately an equal amount of Flow Release or water into each well. The more water or Flow Release you add, the more pastel-like your colors will be. There are a billion different folds (at least), but you can start with a simple accordian fold.

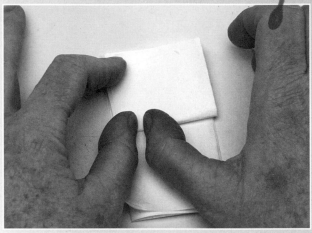

2. Continue Folding

After the first set of folds, turn the paper and fold it the other way in a little packet. Vary this by creating a triangle. I use binder clips to keep the "packets" closed as I fold several sheets of paper while my hands are still clean.

3. Dip in Water

Dunk the packet in water. Remove the clip and squeeze the packet gently to rid it of excess water. The paper should be damp, not dripping.

4. Drop Ink

I've used a pipette to squirt some red ink into one of the corners of my packet. You can also inject some ink by nudging the pipette gently between the folds of paper.

5. Dip Into Ink

Alternatively, you can dip the damp packet, corner by corner, into different colors of ink, gently squeezing the packet to distribute the ink.

6. Apply Ink With Brush

Metallic inks look beautiful around the edges of these papers. Brush ink along the outer edges.

7. Unfold and Add Color

You can open the packet a little bit to add more ink to the interior if you like. (Gently.)

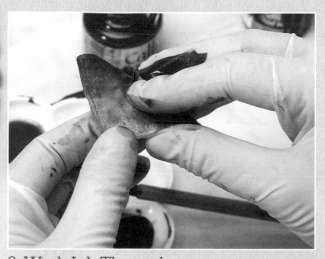

8. Work Ink Through

Gently squeeze the packet to distribute ink, adding more if you'd like or leaving some areas white.

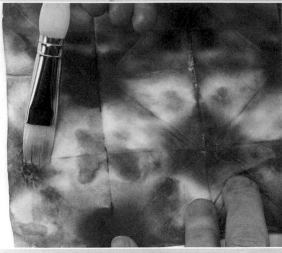

9. Unfold When Dry

After you've finished adding color, place your packet on a paper towel. Close the towel around the packet and blot it well. Allow the packet to dry thoroughly. Patience here! The paper is very fragile when wet and will most definitely tear if you try to unfold it. When the paper is completely dry, unfold it to reveal your pattern. You may want to iron the sheets of paper when dry.

10. Seal With Varnish

I like to coat these lightweight papers with Golden's varnish if I'll be using them in a sewing project.

Stay dry

For variety, try dyeing a dry packet. This results in a crisper design with more whites. Use the same steps as above, omitting step 3.

Blowing Ink

This couldn't be simpler or more satisfyingly random. (This could also be very therapeutic at the end of a hard day!)

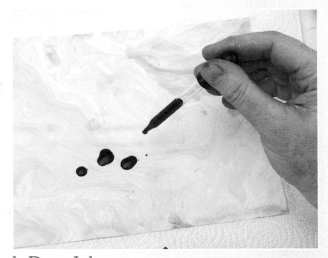

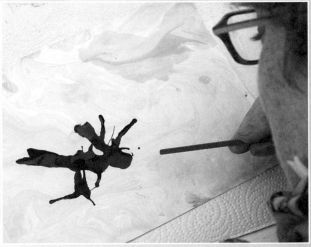

1. Drop Ink

Put a couple of drops of ink on any paper.

2. Blow Ink With Straw

Use a small straw, like a coffee stirrer, and blow through it to move the ink around. That's it!

3. Spritz With Water

This ink was a bit thick so I had to give a spritz to get it moving. Water can also refresh ink that dried a bit when you went to answer the phone.

4. Blow Again

Adding a bit of water will make it easy for the ink to branch out even more.

Debossing

This is a neat trick to use on paper that's been treated with either watercolor or inks.

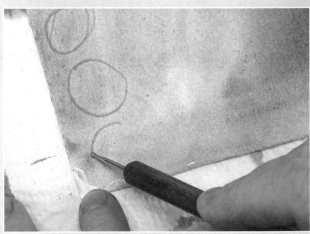

1. Dampen Paper

Spread watercolor or light ink onto a heavyweight art paper.

2. Deboss With Stylus

Using an embossing tool, simply draw designs, words, patterns—whatever—into the paper. You will see that the color becomes concentrated where you've used the tool, making it appear as if you drew or painted the line. An alternative is to deboss the paper first and then add color. The paint will pool in the debossed areas.

Sewing Paper

I love the casual look of hand-sewing, and the feel of the needle and thread against paper is somehow soothing. I think it reminds me of those sewing cards from when I was young. Sometimes though, a machine can be a real timesaver, so I'll sew that way too.

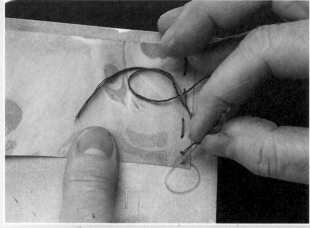

1. Pre-Punch Holes

Set your primary paper and the paper you wish to sew to it on a piece of foam or a mouse pad. If it makes your life easier, you may clip the pages together to secure them. Use a needle tool or a small awl to pre-punch a line of holes where you will be sewing. Here, I am only attaching one side of the paper.

2. Stitch Through Holes

Thread a needle with a couple of strands of embroidery floss and knot one end. Sew through the holes that you punched, either with a back stitch or a running stitch.

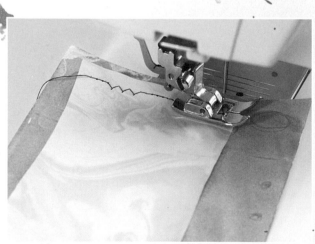

By Machine

Alternatively, you can use a sewing machine to stitch paper together. It's helpful to use a larger stitch rather than a smaller one. A zigzag stitch adds nice texture if you want to mix it up.

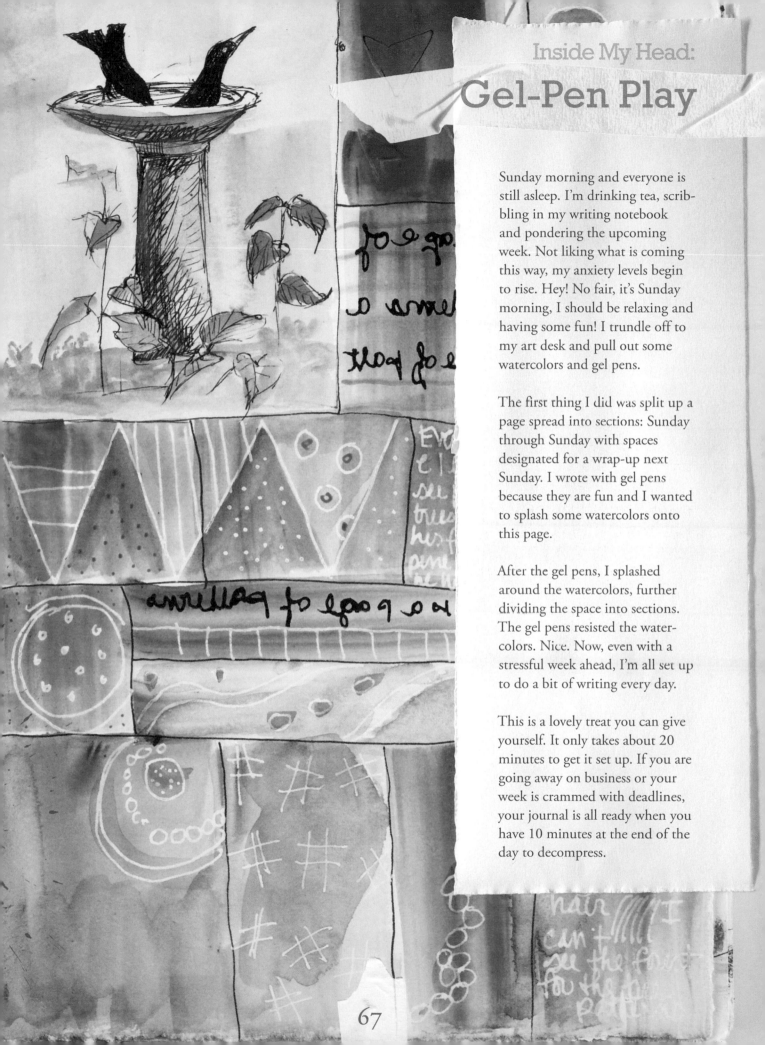

Gel-Pen Play

Sunday morning and everyone is still asleep. I'm drinking tea, scribbling in my writing notebook and pondering the upcoming week. Not liking what is coming this way, my anxiety levels begin to rise. Hey! No fair, it's Sunday morning, I should be relaxing and having some fun! I trundle off to my art desk and pull out some watercolors and gel pens.

The first thing I did was split up a page spread into sections: Sunday through Sunday with spaces designated for a wrap-up next Sunday. I wrote with gel pens because they are fun and I wanted to splash some watercolors onto this page.

After the gel pens, I splashed around the watercolors, further dividing the space into sections. The gel pens resisted the watercolors. Nice. Now, even with a stressful week ahead, I'm all set up to do a bit of writing every day.

This is a lovely treat you can give yourself. It only takes about 20 minutes to get it set up. If you are going away on business or your week is crammed with deadlines, your journal is all ready when you have 10 minutes at the end of the day to decompress.

November

all month the Urge for Doing ho...

the angle of the sun
light up golden and si...
so fragile is their hol...
the trees make that
the shadow stripis
watch and at Nigh...
the bare branches b...
house and th...
...ng off lights,
...breakfast. Why
the Warriors of winte...
stay is dying an...
I will stay ...d ...
blankets to my ...

DEEP IN

Song on the Brain

I'd been listening to the old Joni Mitchell song, "Urge for Going," and it was playing over and over in my head. I've always loved fall and winter—major themes in this track, but this is such a mournful song; why was my mind stuck on this particular soundtrack?

I hauled out the journal and watercolors, inks, water-soluble colored pencils and stamp pads in autumn colors.

I began splashing like a baby in a bathtub. I stopped occasionally to assess the whole thing, writing in pencil, blowing ink, and scribbling here and there with colored pencils.

Yes, I was taking the song way too literally and, I think, after my cathartic splash and scribble, my ever-metaphoric mind was linking the seasons of the song to those of life.

My Space

Where do you live? Or where would you escape to if you could? Although I live in, and adore, my small urban town—filled with neighbors and familiar faces—I dream of thick green forests populated by imaginary animals and birds.

Sometimes I want an entire mountain to myself. I crave empty, eerie, foggy, bleak silence.

This is a good time to let your mind fly as an arm-chair adventurer. Make a journal page of your town and the people you love. Find an imaginary landscape of your own, or some place you've seen or read about that would be the perfect escape spot.

Personal Landscape

This is a good time to go take a walk! Consider taking about 45 minutes and think about where you live and how you feel about this place. Sit outside somewhere and observe the comings and goings of your neighbors. This exercise can be a journal entry about where you really live or it can be about where you would like to escape to sometimes.

With these thoughts, start with spill writing onto the page. As always, be very free with your spill writing. Keep your pen moving. Did any surprises come out?

You can also do some collage spilling here. As with word and color spilling, this activity should feel aerobic. Move quickly and without hesitation. Keep your hands moving at all times! See more in Collage Spilling 102 (page 76).

Gather This

journal

pen (for spill writing)

collage paper scraps

glue stick

gesso

pencil

water-soluble crayons

watercolor

Quick Collage

Allow about a half-hour for this exercise.

1 Take one minute to quickly select some collage paper scraps from your stash. Take a second minute to tear or cut them to size. What size? Just small, manageable pieces that will create some texture when combined together. Don't get hung up on each scrap's size.

2 Now, randomly drop them on the page, one at a time. Glue them down where they drop. If a scrap or two is hanging off the page, that's OK—glue it down. You can trim the page later, if need be.

3 Add some gesso. Yep, gesso *again*. Smear some around over your glued-down scraps. Gesso is the great unifier, in my mind. A thin coat pushes the words and imagery into the background and gives you the freedom to move on and not be boxed in by what you've done so far. (Hey! Is gesso a metaphor for forgiveness?) I love to collage in layers. It may not be evident to the casual observer how many layers are on one page, but *you* will know. They are layers of process: veils of thought one atop another, building to the finale.

Listen to the Page

Pause now. Practice working from your gut and notice if any images or words or quotations are floating into your mind as you see what is developing on your page. As I was building this collage, an image of a mountain just began to occur to me. I quickly drew in a whole range of mountains for myself, using a pencil in the wet gesso.

Leave & Come Back

This is a good time for a break. Let things dry. When you come back to this page spread, try to look at it objectively and with fresh eyes. Do you see anything surprising?

First, take care of any pieces of the collage that may be coming up. Work some bits back down with glue and tear away others. Just get your page relatively flat.

If a large enough piece of the collage came up, rather than fight it, join it! You may want to treat it as a doorway or flap and write something under it. Problem solved.

Add Some Color

1   Time for some color play. I used a combination of Caran d'Ache and watercolor here. With my mountain in mind, I kept the color thin and light at first.

2   Play with texture. I added images from some carved stamps to the bottom of the page, as well as some mark-making with other items. I began to write and draw using a brush and black ink. Don't worry about creating a realistic picture here. The textures and marks that you make may be completely symbolic rather than something to be taken as part of a literal landscape.

3   Not sure what to do? When in doubt, flick some ink! I felt the page needed some oomph and flicked some red ink over the spread. Perfect!

Journal Any New Thoughts

It's never too late to add more writing. Capture how you feel about your finished page on a scrap of paper. I found a scrap of watercolored paper and wrote about how I felt. Fold the scrap however you like and add it as a pull-out or pop-up somewhere that suits you.

Radient st-
azy summer, ked=pu
liquid hot heat, pudd...
cals exotic lush drip...
hot sand cool green...
misty sunrise mornin...
oppressive
heavy o...
leaves

July 18 20

My Space

The Techniques

Spilling words, paint and, in this section, collage, pushes you to work deeper and more intuitively. I hope that you are building up some trust in yourself and that some personal images may be starting to surface. Let them out here. The mantra is, "Put worries in a bubble and blow them away." Work freely and say to yourself, *Ahhh . . . no worries.*

Collage Spilling 102

Collage spilling is another way to spill. It pushes you further into making seemingly random choices. So often, these choices are not random at all but rather intuitive, gently surfacing from deep within. You may not even recognize them at first. Don't scoff—go with it. Practice this and remember to keep your hands busily moving. If your mind starts to interrupt, quietly tell it you are busy right now.

Gather This

- journal
- pen (for spill writing)
- collage paper scraps
- glue stick
- gesso
- brush
- containers of water
- pencil
- scrap paper
- soft carving material (I like Mastercarve)
- craft knife
- permanent pen
- stamp pad, one light colored, one dark
- carving tools (like Speedball—small gouge and large)
- inks and/or acrylic paints, whatever colors you like
- items for making marks
- palette(s) (I save caps from plastic bottles as inkwells)
- paper towel (optional)
- palette knife (optional)
- non-waterproof pen (Zebra Sarasa), black

1. Spill Write

I frequently start my journal pages with spill writing just as a warmup. You can start this way as well.

2. Glue Down Scraps

Perform random acts of collage: Rip, tear and spill paper onto your two-page spread. Glue it where it lands–don't rearrange. (Don't think about not thinking about it, and try not to worry about not thinking.)

3. Add Gesso

One very effective way to get gesso, or any paint, onto your page is to simply squirt some on there. Push the gesso around with your damp brush, creating textures and hills and valleys with pencils or other mark-making tools. Smoosh with your brush, slap your brush into it or wipe some up with a towel or palette knife. Play with the gesso.

4. Sketch in Ideas

Here, I drew into the wet gesso with a pencil, creating my Personal Mountain Range. You may have some image, word or phrase that comes to mind. Leave the page to dry and come back to it later.

Toned down

Sometimes collage elements seem to stand out too much. In order to incorporate them into your artwork, try one or more of the following techniques:

- overlapping the collage elements
- sanding the page
- repeating a shape
- adding a unifying color wash using watercolor, Caran d'Ache, Portfolios, inks, paint or gesso.

Carved Stamps

Rubber stamps are fun to use in your journal, and the process of carving some of your own images makes your journal entries even more personal. Here is my Carving for Dummies, which is all I ever do! If you find yourself loving this process, there are plenty of tutorials, information and classes out there.

1. Sketch Design

Decide upon your design. If this is your first crack at carving, you might want to keep it simple and smallish—maybe 1½" (4cm). Keep in mind that your drawing will be reversed on the finished stamp. Using a pencil, sketch your image onto a piece of paper.

2. Lay Down Graphite

Turn the sketch over and apply a layer of soft graphite to the back of it to make a "carbon."

3. Transfer Sketch to Block

Flip the carbon side down onto the soft carving block and trace over the image using a firm hand and pencil or embossing tool. Lift the paper design up periodically to make sure that the image is transferring.

Stamp-a-Doodle

Keep a page in your journal handy for doodling potential stamp images.

4. Trim Down Block

I've removed the design paper, and you can see the faint pencil transfer, here. Cut the excess carving material away, using a craft knife.

5. Retrace Lines

To make the lines easier to see, use a permanent pen to retrace the image. A permanent pen is best because pencil will eventually smudge off as you're working. (Feel free to skip the transfer process completely and draw simple shapes directly onto the carving material with a permanent pen.)

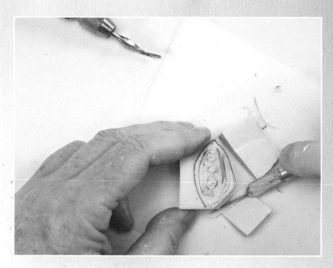

6. Carve Design

Now you are ready to start carving. Begin with a fine blade and work through the details in the center. **Tip:** To carve circles, it's easier to turn the block and keep the blade stationary. After you're done with the fine details, carve off the excess softblock material outside of the image, using a craft knife. Make sure that you create a gentle sloping valley away from the cut. A shelf will break down and weaken your stamp.

Plan B

This is a quick alternative to transferring smaller images to a carving block. An added benefit to this technique is that you don't have to "think in reverse" when drawing—or writing words!

1. Begin with your carving material trimmed to size. After you have your drawing on paper done in pencil, go over it with a Sarasa (or other non-waterproof) pen.

2. Dampen the blank carving block by tapping it on a wet cloth.

3. Press the damp side of the block onto the design drawing done in the non-waterproof pen. (Try not to move the block.)

4. *Voilá!* The drawing will have transferred to the damp block. Allow the transferred image to dry and then retrace over the transferred design with a permanent (waterproof) pen.

7. Test Stamp

Sometimes it is difficult to see where you are in the carving process. If this happens, ink your stamp and test it. Examine both the inked stamp and the stamped image. You'll easily see if more material needs to be carved away.

Here is my first "proof" of my pod image. There was a little bit of material I wanted to remove outside of the image on the right, and the white line on the right seemed a bit wavy.

8. Clean Up and Test Again

If there are parts of the stamp that printed that you feel still need to go away, continue carving and make a second test print. I did a bit more cutting until I was satisfied with the print.

Alternative Mark Making

Take about a half hour to collect mark makers. This is a huge part of the fun in this project. Walk around with a basket and collect anything you think might work and that you don't mind getting ink on—branches, sponges, bottle caps, yarn, ribbons, fabric scraps, cosmetic sponges, regular sponges, clothespins, woodblocks—whatever. Some mark-making items will work better with acrylic paints; some will be more amenable to ink.

Skewer

Skewers are very handy to have in the studio and are lovely writing tools.

Straw

Coffee straws are great for drawing. They can either be dipped into the ink, or you can actually pick up some ink in them by holding your finger over the top and then dropping the ink in a nice messy puddle onto your page. Here, I blew bits of ink out of the straw (always exciting) and bounced the inky straw onto the surface of the paper.

Craft Stick

I like this coffee stirrer a lot! It holds ink well and gives a nice varied line.

Japanese Brush

The supple Japanese brush makes beautiful lettering with a bit of practice. But you don't need to limit its use to letters. It can make lines with a wide variety of thicknesses, too.

Cardboard

This is a hunk of the sleeve from a take-out coffee. I love the scalloped edge. Change the shape with your fingers. Here I used two stampings to create ovals and then the heart shape. You might want to blot excess ink from the cardboard after you dip it, before stamping onto the paper.

Cardstock

Heavy cardstock (such as a hunk of cereal box) is one of my favorites. You can bend and fold the cardboard into any number of shapes and tape it in place. Here I've created a square. When I stamped the second square down, there was a bubble of ink inside the square that burst—a very cool effect!

Ribbon

When working with ribbon, string or trim, you might want to wear gloves to keep your fingers stain-free. Silk ribbon creates a cool print: textural and linear. Dip a length of ribbon into the ink and then work the excess ink out of the ribbon. Experiment with how much ink needs to be removed before printing. Arrange the ribbon on your page, set a paper towel over it (or if you want a print on the other side of the page spread as well, close the page). Brayer over the page or paper towel, then lift it. Remove the ribbon to reveal the print.

Trim

You can experiment with pom-poms and ric-rac in the same manner as the ribbon. Label your experiments so that you can remember what you did.

do an embroidery

poppy
4/11/07

later today I saw a thumb
drive made into a little
chunk of a branch. So th
you see... Technology mee
Nature.

4.
something
ugly. Techno-
logy is so
ugly

April 18 · 2007 ✕✕✕✕✕✕✕✕✕✕✕✕✕✕✕✕✕✕ patterns:

Rocks and Moss. At the Sculpture garden at AAL.
Needed more time. Will have to go back
I like especially
the patterns I
found.
Everything
fabric to me lately.
mbining fabric patterns
very satisfying. And
ways always COLOR. I
re to work in Black and
ite only with words on paper.
as the background. It - B + W -
ever seems finished until
lor is introduced. Will make
ime on weekend in the Mountains to make more sketches. Sneak A

Drawing Games

Doodle Spilling

Give yourself about a half-hour for each of these games. Put on some music—something with a beat. Open your journal and grab a black pen. Begin to doodle, listening to the music and following along. Make curving lines, straight lines, jagged lines. Try not to overlap your lines.

Experiment with different music.

Try out different pens or try pencils.

Try a variation by overlapping the lines this time to get curving, organic shapes.

Abstract Drawing Game

Open your journal and grab a pen.

Draw a curved line from one edge of the paper to the other, three times. Observe the resulting shapes as you use the following directions:

Draw a straight line three times.

Draw one simple shape three times.

Fill in three shapes with patterns, such as cross-hatching, dots, circles, lines (straight or wavy), or organic or geometric shapes.

Using watercolors or colored pencils, fill in three shapes with color.

Repeat any of the above, as desired.

You can use plain printer paper for these games and then make copies of them for collage fodder. Fill them in with color. Fill the spaces with words or images. Collage over them. You get the idea.

Lifeline

Autobiography is such a big, formal word. It implies that the life is over, and this is definitely *not* what I am talking about.

This chapter has you take a look at life in its huge, rambling, unfinished form: building, changing, simplifying, refining, enriching, screwing up and moving on. A life in process, being lived to its fullest degree.

I ran across this quote by Thoreau recently, "If I am not, who will be?"

So first, who am I?

I am mother, wife, sister, aunt, friend, teacher, artist.

I am the worrier and the fixer (sometimes before it's even broken).

I am the soup maker.

I am the yeller.

I am the compulsive one.

I am the colorful one.

I am brutally honest.

I am necessary and meant to fill my small spot.

I am not what people expect of me.

I am not two-dimensional.

I will surprise you and myself with what I am capable of.

Do not put me in a box; I won't fit.

Who are you?

If I Am Not, Who Will Be?

This exercise is about celebration. Honor yourself—good stuff and not-so-good stuff. It's all about you. If you can find a picture of yourself to include, that you consider awful, then you won't worry about messing it up, and you'll be embracing your imperfections. Think about the wabi-sabi you. The Japanese have a custom: When a piece of pottery is broken, it is glued back together; the crack is highlighted with gold and considered beautiful.

Photo Altering

This fun process of altering a photo makes it much easier for me to actually *look* at less-than glamorous pictures of myself. Consider being brave and starting with a photo that you might not ever use on a professional Web site. I started this two-page spread with a picture of myself in a cheshire cat hat, a tuxedo jacket and a marvelous ladybug scarf. (Yes, I wore this outfit out of the house.)

There are all sorts of wonderful photo-altering techniques out there; this is just one simple technique to get you started.

You might feel more comfortable having more than one copy of your photo to play with. Order a few prints of favorite pictures for your stash.

1 Crop your image to the size you want it. Feel free to be neat and use scissors. I just ripped mine down to size.

2 Dip a scrap of superfine (600-grit) sandpaper into water and gently rough up your photo.

3 Now that the photo is damp, an awl can be used to scratch into the surface. I added some stripes on my tuxedo jacket.

Gather This

journal

self-portrait photo for altering (a "real" photo; not an inkjet or laser copy)

sandpaper, 600-grit

container of water

awl or scribe

water-soluble crayons

watercolors

brushes

gesso

tape (such as masking or medical)

graph- or other light-weight paper

glue stick

Copic marker (or similar)

prepainted paper scraps

eyelets and setting tools

white correction fluid, paint or paint pen

black pen

scissors

needle and thread (optional)

fabric strips (optional)

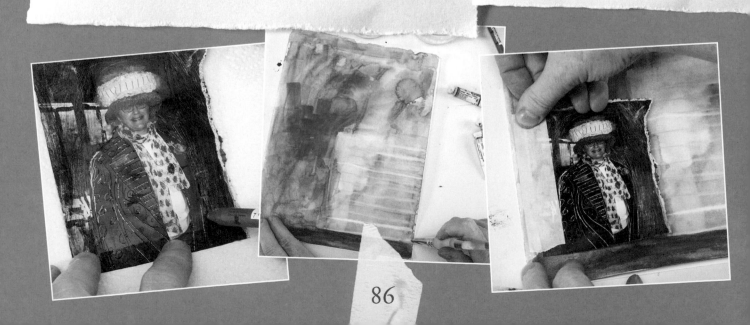

Play With Some Color

Scribbling onto the photo with a water-soluble crayon is a quick way to get some color going. The crayon will stick especially nicely where you have scratched the photo. Rub it in well.

I splashed some watercolors onto my journal page at the same time. Add color in any way that you'd like. I wanted an area on my page that I could write in, so I gessoed a rectangular shape and then drew lines with more white gesso.

Add a Flap (or a Book!)

Flaps are a good way to add dimension to your journal; you can hide some words under them or treat them as a door to another image. I taped the left-hand edge of my picture to the page. If you use paper tape, you can write or color on top of it.

1 Do you have more to say than can be fit under that single flap? Yep, me too. I decided to make the flap into a book. If you'd like to try this, cut a piece of graph paper (or any lightweight paper) a little less than two times the width of the flap.

2 Fold it in half, reopen it and lay it down with the left half on the back of the opened flap.

3 Next make a spine. We'll call this an "interior spine." Cut a long, skinny piece of graph paper 1"–2" (3cm–5cm) longer than the height of your "book." You could use a piece of tape, a fabric strip, or a needle and thread for this. Keep it skinny so that the book can close.

4 Lay the spine along the left edge, aligned with the gutter fold. Glue the top and bottom ends where the spine extends beyond the book.

5 Another way to add dimension and interaction to your page is by making a little pocket using a scrap of painted paper and eyelets. Fold books (pages 109–111) can be tucked into pockets, or you can glue the back cover to your journal page.

Add a Title

I wrote the quote *If I am not, who will be?* in large letters across the top of the page using a black Copic marker. It felt like the lettering needed a little pop, so I added some correction fluid.

I drew black lines on top of the white, rectangular gessoed area, creating a nice shape and making the writting appear as a pattern.

Take a look at the composition on this page. It is a scrapbook-type of format: Label across the top, image on the right and journaling on the left. These stock compositions are easy to fall back on and can make life easier at times.

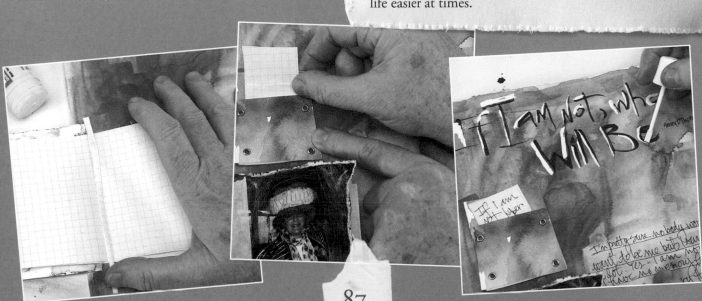

i need to get PasT OveR and just my MY

This is not mo

SELF

Lifeline Altered Journal

Gather This

old book

craft knife

gesso

brush

various paints and collage papers

scissors

glues

gel medium, decoupage medium or PVA

decorative paper

polymer varnish

Stonehenge or other good art paper cut to the height of your book, minus ½" (13cm) and two times the width of the book, minus ½" (13cm), 2 sheets

awl

paperclip

binding needle (or tapestry needle)

waxed linen (bookbinding thread)

heavyweight paper, white

textile paper (see page 100)

embellishments to your heart's content

watercolor pencils or markers

tape

craft stick

glitter glue (optional)

top-loading manila envelope

feather ribbon

transferred image on vellum

brad

pen or pencil

double-stick tape

While you are creating a spread about your own Lifeline, please keep in mind that it is far from over yet. There will always be dreams, hopes and goals to look forward to. These things may be small as well as large, but I hope you'll do a lot of messy spilling and see what emerges from the murk.

Altering an Existing Book

An old book can be given new life in a variety of ways. The entire book can be used in its original form by coating the cover with gesso and painting or collaging over it and then coating the pages with gesso as well before creating new art journaling on them. If you decide to go this route, you may want to glue some of the pages together to create sturdier pages. Other pages can be removed to create more room in the book for chunky embellishments.

When choosing a book, make sure that there is no mildew starting to grow and no moldy smell. Ideally, the pages should bend without cracking and be on the thickish side.

Gessoing over pages is great filler work for a busy week. Just leave the materials sitting out, and as the spreads dry, turn to another spread and gesso some more.

Repurposing a Cover

This process is part altered book and part book-binding. Sometimes you don't want the bulk of a large, existing text block, and you'd rather use your own art-paper spreads anyway, but you want a sturdy, quick-and-easy cover. For this journal, you will start by taking the cover off of an old book, and then you'll sew your own paper pages into its spine. I like the flexibility of this type of journal. I can add in pages or signatures as I go along or fill it with blank signatures now.

1 Open the front cover of your book and stand it up; look down into the spine, between the text block and the spine. You should see a space there.

2 Run a sharp craft knife down where the cover paper (the paper making up the first page and glued to the inside of the cover) meets the text block, along the length of the spine. Repeat with the other cover to completely remove the text block so that you are left with the covers and the spine material that connects them together. (These old text blocks are a great source of collage papers.)

3 Now you can decorate the cover, personalize it and make it your own. Give it a coat of gesso to make repainting easier. Maybe you want to glue images or decorative pieces of paper to the cover. Go for it!

I opened my book completely and laid it flat with the outside covers facing up. I decided to paint the covers over completely—both sides. I made a big handprint on the front cover and painted that in, added a title for my new journal, and embellished it.

Let the outside covers dry and then flip the whole thing over to work on the inside covers.

4 Lay the book opened flat on your worktop with the inside covers facing up. You can use large pieces of paper to completely cover these inside covers or make any kind of collage you'd like.

I decided to cover the inside with decoupage medium and then laid down squares of old book pages, sort of patchwork-style. I did this for both halves of the cover. I stained the paper with a wash of burnt sienna acrylic paint mixed with glazing medium just to give it a softer, more aged look. You can use any kind of aging process that you like, or leave it be.

4 Complete the inside of the cover by cutting a piece of decorative paper approximately 5" (13cm) wide and the height of your book. This paper should completely cover the old spine and overlap the front and back inside covers. I used Japanese paper here both for its beauty and its strength.

If, after drying, the surface feels tacky, coat with polymer varnish.

2A

→ space

VERY OLD BOOK

4 a

spine paper
Same height as Book
Width 4"-5"
Spread glue generously

glue new spine paper over the old spine. Burnish well.

Timeline Strip

A timeline strip is a good project to start with when it comes to filling this journal. This timeline can represent events that happened in the past, with space to fill in events that will occur in the future. If you like, it can be used to mark important events, or you could make it a dream timeline that displays things that you want to do in your future.

1 Cut a long strip of art paper.

2 For the actual timeline element, you may want to draw a line along the edge of the entire width of the paper, or you can glue down a narrow strip of decorative paper, like the Japanese paper I decided to use.

Sewing It Together

When your individual spreads (folios) are complete and you want to sew everying to the spine of your journal cover, begin by making a fold in each piece that you want to add. Together, these folded and stacked papers form what is called a *signature*. When folding your timeline, it doesn't necessarily need to be folded in half, but can be folded at any point along the timeline.

I folded the strip, leaving a stub at the left side of the paper.

1   Stack your folded pages together. Using an awl, punch three holes along the fold through the signature and simultaneously through the spine of the cover. It helps to paperclip the signature being pierced to the cover—a third hand, so to speak.

2   Using a simple pamphlet stitch (see illustration on this page), needle and bookbinding thread, sew this signature into the book.

Pamphlet Stitch

Inner-Creature Paper Dolls

These little dolls are all about randomness. Work intuitively—no planning, please. There is a little bit of a twist in the last step of the making, and you need to trust yourself (and me). No peeking.

I like to use a very simple shape to make these paper dolls. They look a little bit like a cross between traditional Japanese kokeshi dolls and, if you remember, Fisher Price children's toys.

1 Begin by drawing a circle head and some shoulders (no neck needed) onto heavyweight white paper.

2 Leaving a bit of the white paper below the shoulders as overlap, lay a piece of textile paper (see page 100) down and draw out the rest of a simple body.

3 Use scissors to cut out the head/shoulders piece (with the overlap) and the body from the decorative and white papers. Glue the body portion to the overlap area, and the basic doll is done.

4 Now for embellishing! Decorate your doll with sparkles, ribbons, gems, rubber-stamping, yarns, feathers and anything you feel your little doll requires.

I drew some features onto my doll's face with watercolor pencils and washed them in a bit. She looks a bit wistful, doesn't she? I gave her a pointy hat and added some more color. I gave her a bit of green hair. I think she may be a forest gnome.

If you'd like, cut out arms and legs and use brads or eyelets to attach to the body. I didn't feel my gnome needed them.

5 Tape a craft stick on the back of your doll to make it a puppet (and to give it more support if you went overboard on the embellishing).

6 Finally, and most fun of all, browse through a dictionary and randomly find a word to name your dolls. I like to do this after making the doll; you may not think that the random word fits at first, but give it a chance. Glue that name right on your creature. I used glitter glue.

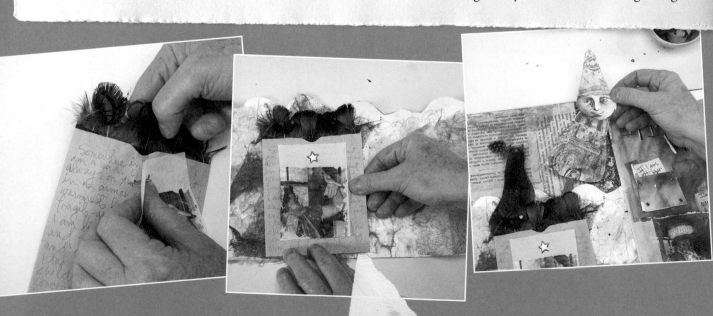

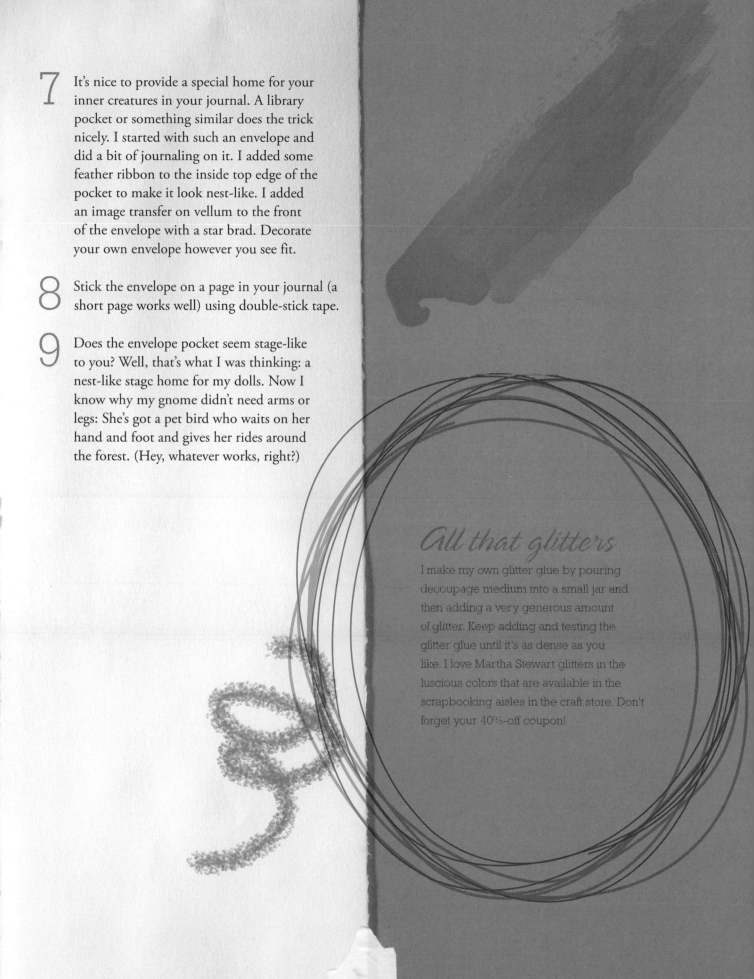

7 It's nice to provide a special home for your inner creatures in your journal. A library pocket or something similar does the trick nicely. I started with such an envelope and did a bit of journaling on it. I added some feather ribbon to the inside top edge of the pocket to make it look nest-like. I added an image transfer on vellum to the front of the envelope with a star brad. Decorate your own envelope however you see fit.

8 Stick the envelope on a page in your journal (a short page works well) using double-stick tape.

9 Does the envelope pocket seem stage-like to you? Well, that's what I was thinking: a nest-like stage home for my dolls. Now I know why my gnome didn't need arms or legs: She's got a pet bird who waits on her hand and foot and gives her rides around the forest. (Hey, whatever works, right?)

All that glitters

I make my own glitter glue by pouring decoupage medium into a small jar and then adding a very generous amount of glitter. Keep adding and testing the glitter glue until it's as dense as you like. I love Martha Stewart glitters in the luscious colors that are available in the scrapbooking aisles in the craft store. Don't forget your 40%-off coupon!

by elimination

Lifeline

The Techniques

There are many things you may wish to include in your Lifeline Journal: A quotations page, a pull-out timeline, mini journals, pockets, tabs and so on—it's really up to you. Here are some tactile techniques to aid you in your creations.

Quotations Page

Dedicating a page (or entire spread) in your journal for favorite quotations makes finding just the right one when you need it quick and easy. Also, this can be a great place to find a prompt when you need one.

Gather This

- journal
- masking fluid
- hand-carved stamps or rubber stamps (simple, bold designs are best)
- lettering brush
- heavyweight paper
- watercolors
- fine-point pen, black
- art papers cut to smaller sizes (9" x 12" [23cm x 30cm] or thereabouts)
- plastic doily (or other item for a textured rubbing)
- crayons
- pigment stamp pads (like Tsukineko StazOn)
- textile paint (I love the Byzantia line of Stewart Gill paints) or acrylics
- stencils (Coffee Break Press)
- paint dauber or stencil brush
- eyelets
- awl
- old mouse pad or craft mat
- setting tool
- hammer
- craft mat

1. Load Stamp With Masking Fluid

Use masking fluid to paint the word *Quotations* across the top of a spread. Also, you can use masking fluid on your hand-carved stamps. Brush it onto the stamp, dabbing off excess fluid if necessary.

2. Stamp Onto Paper

Stamp onto the paper. (Then wash the stamp in water, immediately, to remove the fluid.)

3. Wash With Color

When the fluid is dry, apply a wash of several watercolors over the entire spread.

4. Rub Off Dried Fluid

When the spread is completely dry, rub off the masking fluid to reveal the letters and stamped images.

5. Define With Pen

You can define the letters with a pen if you wish. You now have a spread to record your favorite quotes.

d+white

←Fez

41

Textile Paper

I love the look of hand-decorated paper. Here is a layered example with one technique piled upon the other. You can take it as far as you'd like. I call it textile paper because of the resulting textures and patterns.

You can vary this paper in any way that you'd like. Try the steps in reverse or mix them up just to have some fun and play. Add a layer of writing or an initial layer of a light color of background stamping.

1. Make a Rubbing

Go on a texture hunt around your house, office, yard and neighborhood, and gather items to use for texture. Place a piece of art paper over an item such as the plastic doily used here. Take a crayon (a light color works well) and rub it over the paper to bring out the texture.

You could also take paper and crayon along with you and make rubbings on the go: tree bark, brick, manhole covers, car grills, crackly sidewalks. Put on your texture eyes and go to it.

2. Add Watercolor

The crayon provides a resist for a wash of watercolor. You'll need to let your paper dry at this point, so you may as well do a whole bunch of them for your stash.

3. Stamp Images

For this layer, stamp away using one or more stamps of your choice and stamp right over the crayon and watercolor. Now I'm getting happy with that push-pull of the layers. Are you feeling it?

4. Stencil With Paint

One more layer. Add dimension using paints and a stencil. I love metallic paints on this paper for just the right amount of oomph! I laid a polka dot stencil and pounced some metallic textile paint around.

Eyelets

I love eyelets, but I used to have trouble picking up those tiny things until I came up with this technique. Treat yourself to an hour of experimentation if you've never set an eyelet. It takes a bit of practice to get it just right.

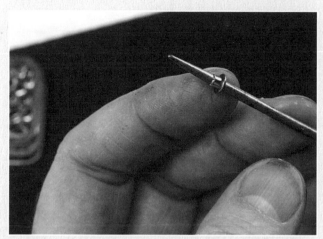

1. Thread Awl With Eyelet

Hold your awl in your dominant hand and slide the eyelet up the length of the shaft until it is snug.

2. Pierce Paper

With the paper laying on a mouse pad (or other cushy pad), use the point of the awl to make a hole.

Eyelets are available in many pretty colors, but I use copper eyelets because the metal is softer and they are easier to set.

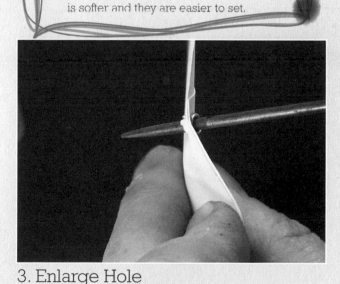

3. Enlarge Hole

Once the hole is started, pick up the paper and hold it vertically. Continue gently pushing the awl in until the eyelet is stuck in the hole. Gently ease the awl out while holding the eyelet firmly in place.

4. Set Eyelet

Lay the paper down on the reverse side, put the point of your setting tool into the tiny opening of your eyelet's shaft, and give it a good whack with your hammer. I usually give it three whacks, but maybe you can do it with one. Remove the setting tool and tap the eyelet with the hammer once more for good measure.

Tabs

I love adding tabs to my journals. For one reason, it looks cool to have stuff sticking out beyond the edges of your book. And, of course, it does help me to quickly locate certain pages for reference.

Shown here are a few ideas for you to make tabs in your book.

Mica

Mica is such a beautiful material. It is simple to use; you simply cut a bit out with a sharp scissors and, despite the cracking sound it makes, it really won't crack. You can crack it if you wish by scoring a line with a craft knife and then breaking it along that line.

When you are piercing a hole in it, use your sharpest awl and a drilling motion to reduce the stress on material.

Pom-Pom Trim

Pom-poms! With heavy gel medium, glue pom-poms onto your journal page. Clip a couple of clothespins to hold the pom-pom to the page until it is dry. I also have a personal fondness for ric-rac.

Milk Jug

I like to cut up well-rinsed milk jugs and use alcohol inks, rubber stamps (with StazOn ink) or permanent markers to decorate them. They make great tabs.

Watercolor Scrap

Rummage through your painted art papers or cardstock. Attach with eyelets, staples, glue or tape.

Silk Ginko Leaf

This nice flat ginko leaf makes a nice tab. With only one eyelet, it can swing around and be hidden in the book and create a little peek-a-boo effect over an image or text.

Manila Tag

Manila tags are so nice and smooth to write or stamp on. I attached one to my page edge with a brad.

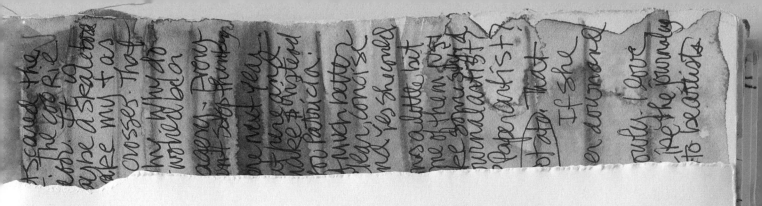

Vellum Tag

I love the whispery-ness of vellum. This is a lovely tag with a silver rim from the scrapbooking section. I attached it with an eyelet.

Sticker

Stickers make great tabs. Lay a sticker on your paper where you'd like it and either fold the excess sticky part back or put a little scrap of paper over the sticky bit.

Binder Ring/Charm

This is a good embellishment for the cover of your book as well. The weight of this tab will tear paper but you can reinforce the area on your page where you want to dangle this charm by backing it with heavy paper or cardboard. Use an awl or Japanese screw punch and slide it into place.

Ribbon

I love to sew in my journal. Here I've added lightly glued ribbon tabs, pierced the sewing holes and then sewed the ribbon in place using embroidery floss.

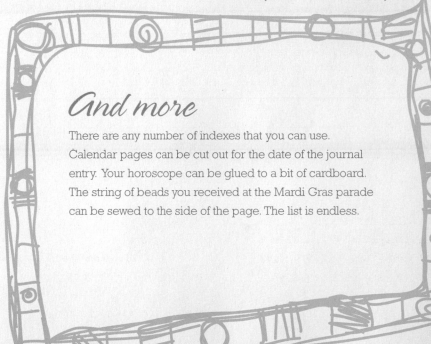

And more

There are any number of indexes that you can use. Calendar pages can be cut out for the date of the journal entry. Your horoscope can be glued to a bit of cardboard. The string of beads you received at the Mardi Gras parade can be sewed to the side of the page. The list is endless.

SiNK

THRUM
THRUM
THRUM

persistent

time

of with

buzz caw trill flap flop flip bing bang tap zing

reset

I NEED VERBS

burst twinkle woke

meticulous
flickering flutter
LAUGH

linger

portly spare concrete cumulous

fly

creat
POWE

whimper

abstract memories

WORDS

verdant green
gray
violet
magenta
orange
ocher
blood red
indigo
rose
crimson

spirit into

holler
ROLL

chirp chum hiss

ds inner outer

HATCH

TWIST

SENSE IMAGINE

Field Trips

No matter where I go, I always have some sort of small notebook (I love my small, traditional Moleskine) with me, tucked into my purse. There's always something that I want to jot down—a color I saw, a shape, a conversation . . . When I'm going away, I pack a few art materials along with my journal in a simple travel kit. Sometimes I pack my journal and travel kit and go for a walk through the nature center or museum. Sometimes I just like to watch the passers-by at the local coffee shop, park or library.

My journal and I love our little "artist dates."

Field Guides

I love making these tiny books as much as I love using them to journal in. One book leads quickly to another, and after a couple of hours, I have a bowl full of them, at the ready, for my next series of outings. The small format makes these easy to slip them into your pocket and be on your way.

There are many ways to make a small booklet. Let's have fun with the two methods here, and then I'm sure more will come to you as you continue to play with paper and other materials. You may want to take just 15 minutes and create one, or take a couple of hours to really play and expand on these ideas.

Accordion Books

Accordion (sometimes referred to as concertina) books are very quick and easy to make. Start with just about any scrap of paper (long and narrow works well) and fold with a serious of alternating folds. (See illustration, below.)

1 I've taken a long piece of previously painted watercolor paper from my stash and folded it in 1" (3cm) sections. You may like 1" (3cm) as well, but if not, feel free to make your folds wherever you like. It's a bit easier if you start by folding the paper in half, first, then fold each half in half and so on.

Gather This

papers (art and/or printer paper)

pens or markers

rubber stamps

stamp pads

printouts of images on transferable papers

gel medium

glue

scissors

cardstock

rubber bands, needle and thread, safety pins (for bindings)

awl

heavyweight black paper

envelopes

pre-painted paper

double-stick tape

needle and thread

plastic canvas (optional)

2 You may want to do a bit of "predecorating" to your pages by embellishing with doodles, stamping or image transfers. These things can help inspire you when you actually go to journal in them out in the field. I added a gel transfer of a pod drawing to one end of the paper and used a carbon transfer to add some flowers to the other. I love those Japanese cherry blossoms! Feel free to add whatever embellishments you'd like, but keep them simple so you'll have plenty of space on the pages for writing, drawing and perhaps adding more transfers after your trip.

3 After the page was completely dry, I refolded it. I measured out the size for the cover and cut that from more painted paper. To make a cover for your accordion, use this formula to determine the size:

Cover width: width of the folded paper (× 2) + about a ¼"(6mm)

Cover height: height of the folded paper + about a ¼"(6mm)

Fold the cover in half.

4 I glued the first and last sections of the accordian to the inside of the front and back of the folded cover. You may do the same, or you may choose to just glue one section of the accordian to the one half of the cover so that you can still pull the accordion out and work on the long strip.

5 If you like, add a title to the front cover. I embellished the front cover of my book with a image transfer and rubber stamped the words *Field Trip*, *No.* and *Date*.

Pamphlet Books

Ready to try making another kind of book? Here are a few simple pamphlet books with unusual bindings.

Basic Technique

1 Select paper that you want for the pages (also known as the text block) and cut several to approximately the same size. Fold the pages in half and stack them together to make a signature.

2 For a cover, cut coverstock (cardstock or other heavier-weight material) two times as wide as the folded text block plus about ¼" (6mm) and to the height of your text block plus about ¼" (6mm).

3 Fold the cover over the signature and along the fold. Secure with a rubber band. Done!

Variations

Binding choices for these little folded books are plentiful. I tried giving one a safety-pin binding. I pierced two holes through the folded stack with an awl and inserted a safety pin. Feel free to embellish the safety pin or perhaps you prefer the Zen appeal.

Looking for something more understated? After poking three holes through the spine of the pamphlet, insert a little brad through each hole and splay the ends inside of the fold to keep the book together.

Then of course there's my famous duct tape book! Cut two pieces of cardboard for your covers. Cut a bunch of signatures two times the width of the covers and the same height. Pull off a piece of duct tape twice as long as the height of your book plus 2" (5cm) and lay it sticky side up on your work table. Lay the covers, right side down and centered, along the length of the tape. Leave approximately ½" (13mm) between the covers. Bring the bottom of the tape up and burnish. Bring the top of the tape down and burnish. Make sure any sticky duct tape is covered. Use rubber bands or binding thread to secure the signatures.

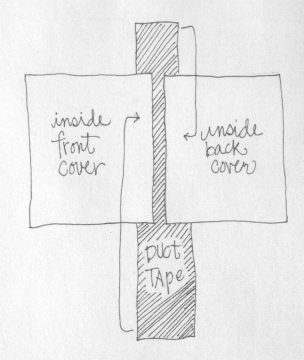

Accordion Spine Journal With Flags

This is a takeoff of a flag book.

1. Begin with an accordion-folded strip that is whatever height you like and has folded segments that are about 1" (3cm) wide. I used some heavyweight black paper.

2. Cut envelopes (either ones you create from prepainted paper or commercial ones) to the height as your accordian and whatever width you want for pages. Cut some painted papers the same size or smaller, if you'd like, for additional pages.

3. Using double-stick tape, adhere the envelopes and the painted pages to alternating sides of the accordion folds, with the openings of the envelopes facing out.

4. It's easy to make a slip cover for your flag book. I decided to try using a bit of plastic canvas. I spray-painted it black and then folded it in half. I whip-stitched the sides together and then cut out a thumb hole at the opening end. This is a nice, sturdy envelope to keep my field-trip findings safe and sound.

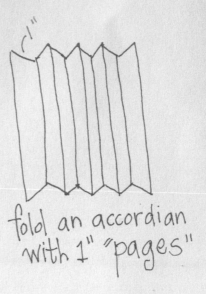

fold an accordian with 1" "pages"

Glue envelopes and painted paper to 1" "pages"

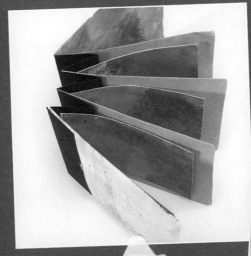

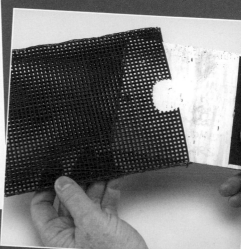

on vacation
I think
very in
for im
get au
it is a

funny
I ca
tr

flowe

summer 2002

Would you Like AN Adventure

CHAPTER

I have a tendency to just stay home with Chopin, art, sewing, reading, and t.v. I go for walks to the gym. I take big physi... My idea of an ...es looking for a book on the lower shelves at the library. Perhaps it is enough risk to make art and show it. To put myself out there for scrutiny by a load of people. I don't ... know. Maybe my ... "adventure" energy gets used is too much. that does make sense

making cooking watching ...ks and never... ...cal risks ...adventure

Field Trips

The Techniques

When you are first learning these techniques, start out with small images to make things easier on yourself. A smooth heavy art paper such as Stonehenge works best. Tags, manila and cardstock work well, too, especially after a smooth coating of paint or gel medium. Spend some time practicing and experimenting.

Inkjet Transfer

This method makes beautiful transfers. They look almost like Polaroid transfers.

On White Paper

1. Make a Tab
Using your inkjet printer, print out your chosen image to transfer, onto transparency paper or JetPrint. Here I've cut out an image of the Temple of Diana. I left about ½" (13mm) excess on one side. Find the slightly sandy side of the paper—that is the image side. Fold the excess area back away from the image side to give yourself a little handle and to make sure you are working with the image-side of the transfer down.

Gather This

ink jet printer (I use an Epson printer with DURAbrite inks)

image printed on transparency paper (Apollo) or Jet Print Photo Multi-Project Glossy paper

gel medium

paper to receive the transfer

brayer, bone folder (burnishing)

brush, water, rag

black paper

interference paint

fine-mist water bottle (I like the Ranger brand's version)

embossing tool

wax paper

tape

soft graphite pencil

Transfer tips

When you go to load your printer with transparency paper, pay attention to which side is up. You want your image to print on the rougher side. (See the manufacturer's directions). There are a couple of tiny things I do that may differ from techniques you've seen or read about in the past that I find ensure a good transfer.

If you are transferring to soft or lightweight paper, you will get the best results if you coat the receiving paper with gel medium and allow it to dry.

2. Apply Gel Medium

Holding the image by the handle, coat it with some gel medium. I use my finger to spread it completely and evenly over the image. Allow it to set up for a moment.

3. Burnish

Lay the image, gelled side down, onto your receiving paper (your journal). Gently smooth to remove any bubbles and ensure contact with receiver paper, using a bone folder or a brayer.

4. Peel Off Film

Now, this is important: Leave the image to set for two to five minutes. Let the gel medium do the work for you. Check that your image has transferred by lifting a corner of the transparency. You may need to burnish lightly again. Gently lift the transparency away from your image. Admire.

Sticky situation?

If your image is sticking to your support paper, you may not have added enough gel medium. If your image smears and distorts when you brayer over it in step 3, you may have too much gel medium. Spend some time practicing with a pile of these images.

What to transfer?

I love to transfer black-and-white line drawings. You can also use clip art, copies of bits of text, or manipulated photos. Look through your journals for images.

Over Interference Paint (Variation)

1. Paint Paper

Prepare a piece of black paper by applying a thin smooth coat of interference paint and let the paint dry.

2. Make Transfer

Using steps 1–4 from above, create an image transfer. (I used this kind of image transfer on my Field Trip journal.)

Water Transfer

This image makes more aged, ethereal transfers. You can easily write and paint over them.

1. Spray Image

Print out your image onto the JetPrint paper. Cut it down to size, leaving extra space for a "handle." Spray both the image and the receiving paper with a fine mist.

2. Transfer to Paper

Set the image face down on your receiving paper and roll over the back of the image with a brayer. Leave it for a few seconds, letting the water work its magic. Check the transfer by peeling back just a corner before peeling off the entire sheet. If it looks good, peel away; if not, try brayering it again.

Carbon Paper Transfer

While this may seem a bit more tedious than other transfers, it brings some great side effects. Anyone can do these transfers, at 3AM, without the use of any special mediums or equipment—just you and your pencil (or chalk or oil pastel). Another benefit is that it will help you to improve your drawing skills.

1. Apply Graphite

Start with a simple drawing (or clip art). Cover the back of your drawing/tracing with an even layer of soft graphite pencil in the areas directly over the image's lines.

Other ideas

To transfer oil pastel, trace the back side of the drawing, with one stroke of pastel over the lined areas to be transferred. The pastel stick is typically wide enough that this is easy to hit your mark. Try brushing watercolor over your oil-pastel transfer. The transfer will act as a resist.

Another idea is to use white charcoal pencil on the backside of the image, just like you laid down the graphite, and then transfer your image to a piece of dark paper.

2. Burnish Over Image

Place the carboned side down onto your receiver paper; you may want to tape it in place to hold it securely. Now trace the image again. I like to use an embossing tool for this; it rolls nicely over the line. *Voila!*

3. Lift Off Paper

Lift your drawing/tracing to check your transfer. If you like, you can now color in the image with watercolors or colored pens.

Wax Paper Resist

The use of simple wax paper to create a resist for watercolor couldn't be easier, and you can have a lot of fun with this. Don't limit yourself to imagery; try using this technique with actual writing as well!

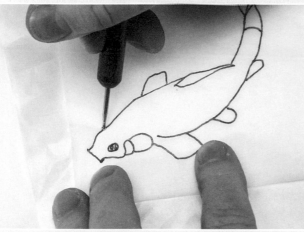

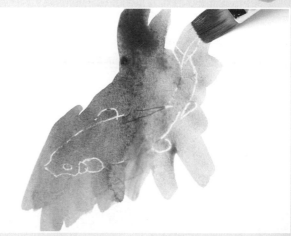

1. Trace Over Image

A simple variation on the carbon transfer is to substitute waxed paper. Lay down your receiving paper, then a piece of wax paper. Again, it is a good idea to tape these layers down. Lay your image on top of the waxed paper and, using an embossing tool, trace over the image. This will deposit a line of water-resistant wax onto your receiving paper.

2. Wash Color Over Resist

You may not be able to see the wax that transferred onto the paper, but when you use some watercolor magic over the top—ta-da! The wax acts as a nice resist.

Field Trips Traveling Kit

One of the reasons I love water-colors so much is that they travel well. I pack my little tin-handled case with my watercolor palette, two water brushes, a spray mister, scissors and gluestick, pen and pencil, and, of course, my journal.

When my husband and I traveled to Rome for a whirlwind five-day anniversary trip, I brought only this case and included a handful of Derwent Inktense watercolor pencils, instead of the watercolor palette and a small-sized Moleskine sketchbook. Perfect! Even during the wait at airports and the plane ride, I journaled while my husband caught up on his zzzs. During our cavorts about the Eternal City, I just kept my notebook and pen with me. This journal is a wonderful keepsake of a very special trip and includes a drawing by my husband of our airplane and a note from our waiter at our 30th anniversary dinner. It's in Italian, and he wouldn't tell us what it meant!

Consider how you might put together your own traveling kit. I find it's best to have supplies dedicated to this grab-and-go box so that you don't need to worry about switching materials back and forth at a moment's notice.

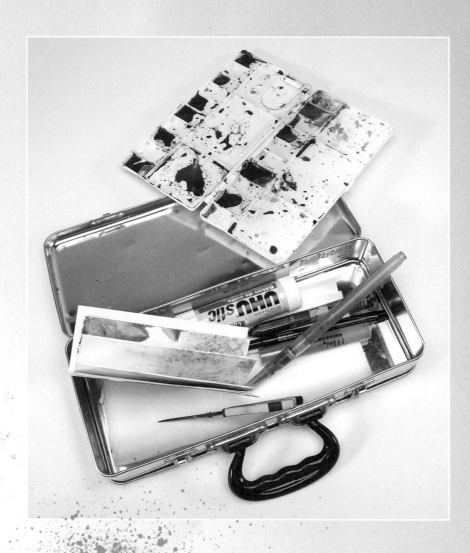

Words for Spilling

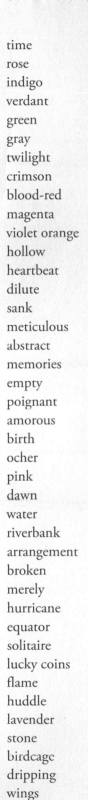

time	many-eyed	starlight	love	think	press
rose	sparse	grids	live	write	sense
indigo	surprise	lines	loving	see	stir
verdant	persistent	shadows	bitter	trailing	lift
green	tap	vision	seeming	replaced	illuminate
gray	zing	version	seems	woke	scratch
twilight	holler	flit	ending	awaken	flare
crimson	trill	grin	begging	playing	strike
blood-red	chirp	twerp	beggar	escape	twist
magenta	chum	impending	descends	cloying	stow
violet orange	hiss	journey	descending	dance	gripping
hollow	portly	atmosphere	descent	pantomime	thrust
heartbeat	spare	silver	betrayed	ferry	flashing
dilute	concrete	gold	rise	flood	rolling
sank	cumulous	copper	rising	ascend	swim
meticulous	clouds	flight	rose	vigilant	grow
abstract	inner	tender	thud	burst	burst
memories	outer	willow	thumping	twinkle	running
empty	topography	curving	beating	flutter	murmuring
poignant	pale	feather	ink	want	shouting
amorous	spirit	perch	sink	need	sweeps
birth	light	weightless	wash	exposed	laughing
ocher	dark	dream	painting	immersed	crying
pink	day	window	coloring	continuing	rushed
dawn	night	door	rejoice	hunger	drowned
water	compass	house	lament	encompassing	broke
riverbank	bend	sparking	deeply	feed	lie
arrangement	wildflowers	flickering	deepened	ravish	bubble
broken	tug	broken	belonging	remember	bubbling
merely	feeble	lean	belongs	demand	dressed
hurricane	tree	thought	count	urgent	drumming
equator	branch	sparkle	calling	release	whisper
solitaire	leaf	capture	prepare	linger	spill
lucky coins	grass	butterfly	preparing	wish	naïve
flame	roll	bird	cautionary	longing	velvet
huddle	hills	cat	caution	hopeless	smooth
lavender	river	mouse	pour	hopeful	blind
stone	stream	gallop	dumping	sit	snow
birdcage	ocean	horse	taste	reject	
dripping	sky	imagine	touch	leaving	
wings	star	dream	desire	taking	

Quick & Dirty Prompts

This list is for those days when you long to do something creative but you're having blank-page issues. Read through several of these ideas until you find something that speaks to you, or close your eyes and point to one idea.

You can break down these "jobs" into 5-, 10-, 20- or 60-minute bits of time.

Do some spill writing in your journal. How was your day? Or, how would you like it to be?

Do some color spilling in your journal.

Play a doodle game in your journal. (See page 83.)

Make a chart on one page of your journal to chart your moods for the week: sad, anxious, tired, in balance, feeling good, feeling great, dancing a jig.

Randomly pick a word from the dictionary. Write it at the top of a journal page. Write or draw what this word brings to your mind.

Make a healing page for yourself or someone you love who may be sick or struggling with a problem. Write good wishes frequently.

Create a Words page—a page you can use for prompts when you need a good word. Open a two-page spread and spill some paint. While it is drying, go through magazines with good writing or make copies of poetry (or print them out on the computer). Cut out words that you like and paste them onto your page. Don't forget to index this page with a tab. (See page 102.)

Found poetry is fun and has the best words! Flip through old books of poetry and clip out the words that appeal to you. Arrange them into a new poem of your own.

Set up a spread in your journal for Symbol Drawing. You did tons of symbol drawing when you were a child, before someone told you that you couldn't draw for beans. Embrace your inner kindergartener and go there again. These drawings are not meant to be DaVinci-style; they should help you to begin to build a vocabulary of small things you'd like to be able to make simple drawings of—drawings that can serve to symbolize your thoughts throughout your journal.

Examples: leaves, flowers, trees, birds, squirrels, dogs, cats, houses, buildings, cars, a lightbulb, a lamp, kitchen items.

Prep your watercolor palette.

Get a stack of magazines that are on their way to the recycling bin. Quickly go through the magazines, ripping out any pages that appeal to you. Keep the pages in a file folder.

Go through your file folder of magazine tear sheets:

Think about the word *color* and pull pages with colors you love. Cut out sample colors. Glue them all down to a journal page.
Substitue the word *color* with:
images
or
text
or
pattern

You can keep these torn-out bits in envelopes in your journal for future inspiration.

Go through photographs and choose some that you are drawn to. Take them to drugstore to make copies.

Shop for transparency paper and other specialty papers.

Prepare and organize digital images on your computer. Stick everything into a virtual folder so it will be easy to print them out.

Print them out!

Tear down parent-size sheets of paper.

Gesso over a page spread in your journal.

Creative Aid:
Quotations

Here are some great quotes for you to print out on sticker paper or use as general inspiration.

Sometimes I've believed as many as six impossible things before breakfast.

—Lewis Carroll

Everywhere I go, I find a poet has been there before me.

—Sigmund Freud

I like trees because they seem more resigned to the way they have to live than other things do.

—Willa Cather

As the poet said, "Only God can make a tree"—probably because it's so hard to figure out how to get the bark on.

—Woody Allen

Inside myself is a place where I live all alone and that's where you renew your springs that never dry up.

—Pearl Buck

Rivers know this: There is no hurry. We shall get there some day.

—*Pooh's Little Instruction Book* by A. A. Milne

Upon those who step into the same rivers different and ever different waters flow down.

—Heraclitus of Ephesus

Tell all the Truth but tell it slant.

—Emily Dickinson

If you asked me what I came into this world to do, I will tell you. I came to live out loud.

—Emile Zola

Happiness is the fine and gentle rain that penetrates the soul, but which afterwards gushes forth in springs of tears.

—Maurice Guerin

Behind every fear is a wish.

—Unknown

Nothing is always a good thing to do and a clever thing to say.

—Will Durant

Fear nothing but the failure to experience you true nature.

—Dogen Zenji

Always listen to experts. They'll tell you what can't be done and why. Then do it.

—Robert Heinlein

Life is a great big canvas and you should throw all the paint you can on it.

—Danny Kaye

I say beware of all enterprises that require new clothes, and not rather a new wearer of clothes.

—Henry David Thoreau

When anger rises, think of the consequences.

—Confucius

A positive attitude may not solve all your problems, but it will annoy enough people to make it worth the effort.

—Herm Albright

Complaining is good for you as long as you're not complaining to the person you're complaining about.

—Lynn Johnston

A strong positive mental attitude will create more miracles than any wonder drug.

—Patricia Neal

I see my body as an instrument rather than an ornament.

— Alanis Morissette

The cure for boredom is curiosity. There is no cure for curiosity.

—Dorothy Parker

So you see, imagination needs moodling—long, inefficient, happy idling, dawdling and puttering.

—Brenda Ueland

To live a creative life, we must lose our fear of being wrong.

—Joseph Chilton Pearce

Better to write for yourself and have no public than to write for the public and have no self.

—Cyril Connolly

Hate no one; hate their vices, not themselves.

—J. G. C. Brainard

Resources

There is a ton of great information on these Web sites. Look for the products in local, small art supply stores and craft stores. We want to keep those folks around for those times that you run out of gesso in the middle of a project (and all the other altruistic reasons).

Golden Artist Colors
acrylic paints and mediums
www.goldenpaints.com

Winsor & Newton
watercolors, mediums and brushes
www.winsornewton.com

Ranger Ink & Innovative Craft Products
white Inkssential pen
www.rangerink.com

Tsukineko
Stayz-On permanent ink pads
www.tsukineko.com

I've found the following Internet sites to have excellent service.

Artist Cellar for Stewart Gill fabric paints.
www.artistcellar.com

Coffee Break Design for eyelets and stencils. To order you need to go to the Web site, download the form and order via mail, but they offer great stuff, reasonably priced.
www.coffeebreakdesign.com

Collage Closet carries JetPrint Photo and Imaging Paper for ink-jet transfers even though the manufacturer has ceased making this paper.
www.collagecloset.com

SkyBluePink is just for fun: toys, papers, collage kits at very reasonable prices.
www.skybluepink.com

Volcano Arts carries bookbinding supplies as well as eyelets and setters. Loads of tools here.
www.volcanoarts.biz

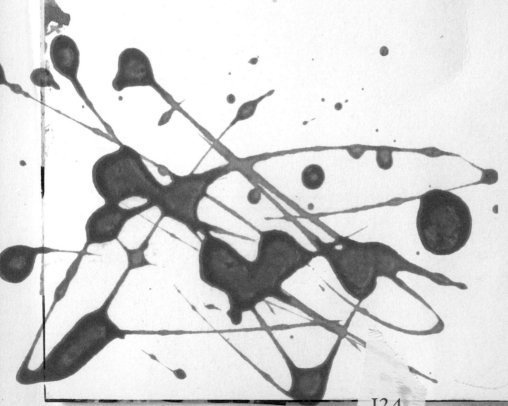

A List of Books I Find Inspiring

Self-Help

Make Your Creative Dreams Real by SARK, Fireside, 2005

Writing

Bird by Bird by Anne Lamott, Anchor, 1995

Writing Down the Bones by Natalie Goldberg, Shambhala, 1986

Poemcrazy by Susan Goldsmith Wooldridge, Three Rivers Press, 1997

A Picture Is Worth 1,000 Words by Phillip Sexton, Writer's Digest Books, 2008

Inspiration

Art & Soul: Notes on Creating by Audrey Flack, Peguin, 1991

The Art Spirit by Robert Henri, Basic Books, 1984

Journal of a Solitude by May Sarton, W.W. Norton & Co., 1992

1000 Journals Project by Someguy and Kevin Kelly, Chronicle Books, 2007

Spilling Open by Sabrina Ward Harrison, Villard, 2000

Drawing From Life: The Journal as Art by Jennifer New, Princeton Architectural Press, 2005

Inspiration and Technique

Kaleidoscope by Susanne Simanaitis, North Light Books, 2007

Artists' Journals and Sketchbooks by Lynne Perrella, Quarry Books, 2004

The Decorated Page by Gwen Diehn, Lark Books, 2003

Make Your Mark by Margaret Peot, Chronicle Books, 2004

Living Out Loud by Keri Smith, Chronicle Books, 2003

Wreck This Journal by Keri Smith, Perigee Trade, 2007

Index

Diana Trout is a painter, book artist and teacher. She studied painting at the University of the Arts and Pennsylvania Academy of the Fine Arts in Philadelphia.

She has shown her work at craft shows and galleries in the Philadelphia area, New York and New Jersey. Diana has taught classes and workshops in painting, journaling, general art and book arts and has taught origami to children and adults at art centers, libraries, national venues and from her studio.

Diana has two kids and lives in the little town of Glenside, with her husband, cat, and a bunch of birds and squirrels.

Contact her at:
www.DianaTrout.com
www.DianaTrout.blogspot.com

photo: Arthur Alexion

←Fez

41

Indulge Your Creative Side With These Other F+W Media Titles

Taking Flight
Kelly Rae Roberts

In *Taking Flight*, you'll find overflowing inspiration—complete with a kindred spirit, in author and mixed-media artist Kelly Rae Roberts. Join her on a fearless journey into the heart of creativity as you test your wings and learn to find the sacred in the ordinary, honor your memories, speak your truth and wrap yourself in the arms of community. Along the way, you'll be inspired by step-by-step techniques, thought-provoking prompts and quotes, and plenty of eye candy—pages and pages of the author's endearing artwork, along with the varied works of the contributors.

ISBN-10: 1-60061-082-X
ISBN-13: 978-1-60061-082-0
paperback • 128 pages • Z1930

Exhibition 36
Susan Tuttle

Jam-packed with visual eye candy, *Exhibition 36* features a plethora of artistic techniques, tips and inspiration from 36 amazing contributing artists. This virtual gallery includes "guest speakers," hands-on workshops and plenty of full-color food for thought. Whether you're looking for painting tips, advice for facing your artistic fears, new tricks for creating digital art or inspiring stories of the challenges artists just like you face, you'll find something of value on every page of this amazing collection of creative food for the soul.

ISBN-10: 1-60061-104-4
ISBN-13: 978-1-60061-104-9
paperback • 144 pages • Z2065

Creative Awakenings
Sheri Gaynor

What if you could unlatch the doors to your heart and allow yourself to explore hopes and dreams that you haven't visited for a very long time? *Creative Awakenings* is the key to opening those doors, showing you how to use art-making to set your intentions. Creativity coach Sheri Gaynor will be your guide through the mileposts of this exciting journey. You'll learn how to create your own Book-of-Dreams Journal and a variety of mixed-media techniques to use within it. A tear-out Transformation Deck will aid you in setting your intentions. You'll also get inspiration from 12 artists who share their own experiences and artwork created with the Art of Intention process.

ISBN-10: 1-60061-115-X
ISBN-13: 978-1-6006-115-5
paperback • 160 pages • Z2122

These books and other fine North Light titles are available at your local craft retailer, bookstore or online supplier, or visit us at www.mycraftivity.com.